Weaving It Together

Connecting Reading and Writing

MILADA BROUKAL

THOMSON ™

HEINLE

Australia • Canada • Mexico • Singapore • United Kingdom • United States

THOMSON
HEINLE

Weaving It Together: Connecting Reading and Writing,
Book 2/Second Edition
Milada Broukal

Publisher, Adult and Academic ESL: James W. Brown
Senior Acquisitions Editor: Sherrise Roehr
Sr. Developmental Editor: Ingrid Wisniewska
Sr. Production Editor: Maryellen Killeen
Sr. Marketing Manager: Charlotte Sturdy
Sr. Print Buyer: Mary Beth Hennebury
Editorial Assistant: Audra Longert
Contributing Writer (Video Activities): Barbara Gaffney

Project Manager: Lifland et al., Bookmakers
Compositor: Parkwood Composition
Photography Manager: Sheri Blaney
Photo Researcher: Susan Van Etten
Illustrator: Ashley Van Etten
Cover Designer: Rotunda Design/Gina Petti
Interior Designer: Carole Rollins
Printer: Transcontinental Printing

Printed in Canada
7 8 9 10   06

For more information contact Heinle, 25 Thomson Place, Boston, Massachusetts 02210 USA, or you can visit our Internet site at http://www.heinle.com

For permission to use material from this text or product contact us:
Tel   1-800-730-2214
Fax   1-800-730-2215
Web   www.thomsonrights.com

Library of Congress Cataloging-in-Publication Data

Broukal, Milada.
    Weaving it together: connecting reading and writing/Milada Broukal.
        p. cm.
    Includes bibliographical references.
    Contents: Bk. 2. High beginning level
    ISBN 0-8384-4808-9
    1. English language—Textbooks for foreign speakers. I. Title.

PE1128 .B7154 2003
428.2'4—dc21   2002032930

Photo credits: Cover: (top) Bonnie Kamin/Index Stock Imagery; (bottom) Carl Rosenstein/Index Stock Imagery. p. 1: (left) © AP/Wide World Photos; (top right) © Bettmann/CORBIS; (bottom right) © AP/Wide World Photos. p. 2: © Zeta Visual Media–Germany/Index Stock Imagery, Inc. p. 15: (left) © Bettmann/CORBIS; (right) © AP/Wide World Photos. p. 29: © FotoKIA/Index Stock Imagery, Inc. p. 30: (left) © Getty Images; (right) © Getty Images. p. 55: © Frank Leather; Eye Ubiquitos/CORBIS. p. 56: © Pat Almasy/CORBIS. p. 66: © Patrick Ward/CORBIS. p. 79: (left) © Mathew Mendelsohn/CORBIS; (top right) © Bettmann/CORBIS; (bottom right) © Jim Lake/CORBIS. p. 80: © Craig Hammell/CORBIS. p. 90: © CORBIS. p. 101: (top left) © Bettmann/CORBIS; (top right) © Archivo Iconografico S.A./CORBIS; (middle left) © Flip Schulke/CORBIS; (middle right) © Bettmann/CORBIS; (bottom left) © Ulrike Welsch; (bottom right) © Bettmann/CORBIS. p. 103: © Getty Images/PhotoDisc. p. 104: © A&J Verkaik/CORBIS. p. 115: (left) © Rick Raymond/Index Stock Imagery; (right) © Jim Zuckerman/CORBIS. p. 127: © Bettmann/CORBIS. p. 128: © Getty Images. p. 139: © Roger Ressmeyer/CORBIS. p. 153: © John Neubauer/PhotoEdit. p. 154: © Michael Newman/PhotoEdit. p. 166: © CORBIS. p. 179: © Massimo Listri/CORBIS. p. 180: © Michelle Garrett/CORBIS. p. 185: © Buddy Mays/CORBIS.
Text credit: p. 181: "This is Just to Say" by William Carlos Williams, from COLLECTED POEMS: 1909–1939, VOLUME I, copyright © 1938 by New Directions Publishing Corp. Reprinted by permission of New Directions Publishing Corp. and Carcanet Press Limited.

Brief Contents

Weaving It Together 2 Contents

To the Teacher

Rationale

Weaving It Together, Book 2, is the second in a four-book series that integrates reading and writing skills for students of English as a second or foreign language. The complete program includes the following:

Book 1—Beginning Level

Book 2—High Beginning Level

Book 3—Intermediate Level

Book 4—High Intermediate Level

The central premise of *Weaving It Together* is that reading and writing are interwoven and inextricable skills. Good readers write well; good writers read well. With this premise in mind, *Weaving It Together* has been developed to meet the following objectives:

1. To combine reading and writing through a comprehensive, systematic, and engaging process designed to integrate the two effectively.
2. To provide academically bound students with serious and engaging multicultural content.
3. To promote individualized and cooperative learning within moderate-to large-sized classes.

Over the past few years, a number of noted researchers in the field of second language acquisition have written about the serious need to integrate reading and writing instruction in both classroom practice and materials development. *Weaving It Together* is, in many ways, a response to this need.

Barbara Kroll (1993), for example, talks of teaching students to read like writers and write like readers. She notes: "It is only when a writer is able to cast himself or herself in the role of a reader of the text under preparation that he or she is able to anticipate the reader's needs by writing into the text what he or she expects or wants the reader to take out from the text." Through its systematic approach to integrating reading and writing, *Weaving It Together* teaches ESL and EFL students to understand the kinds of interconnections that they need to make between reading and writing in order to achieve academic success.

Linda Lonon Blanton's research (1992) focuses on the need for second language students to develop authority, conviction, and certainty in their writing. She believes that students develop strong writing skills in concert with good reading skills. Blanton writes: "My experience tells me that empowerment, or achieving this certainty and authority, can be achieved only through performance—through the act of speaking and writing about texts, through developing individual responses to texts." For Blanton, as for Kroll and others, both reading and writing must be treated as composing processes. Effective writing instruction must be integrally linked with effective reading instruction. This notion is at the heart of *Weaving It Together.*

Organization of the Text

Weaving It Together, Book 2, contains eight thematically organized units, each of which includes two interrelated chapters. Each chapter begins with a reading, moves on to a set of activities designed to develop critical reading skills, and culminates with a series of interactive writing exercises.

Each chapter contains the same sequence of activities:

1. **Pre-reading activity and key vocabulary:** Each chapter is introduced with a photograph, accompanied by a set of discussion questions and a vocabulary matching exercise. The purpose of the pre-reading activity is to prepare students for the reading by activating their background knowledge and encouraging them to call on and share their experiences. The purpose of the key vocabulary is to acquaint them with the words that appear in the reading. This vocabulary exercise can be done before or after the reading.

2. **Reading:** Each reading is a high-interest passage related to the theme of the unit. Selected topics include Delicacies, Killer Bees, and Robots. The final unit contains readings from literature.

3. **Vocabulary:** Four to eight key vocabulary words or phrases appear in bold type in each reading passage. In the vocabulary exercises that follow the passage, students practice using these words. There are two types of vocabulary exercises. The first one, *Meaning,* uses the new words in the context in which they were used in the reading. The second one, *Vocabulary Activity,* helps students to use the words in new contexts. The vocabulary items then serve as a useful resource for students when they are writing their own sentences on the same theme.

4. **Comprehension:** There are two types of comprehension exercises. The first, *Looking for the Main Ideas,* concentrates on a general understanding of the reading. This exercise may be done after a first silent reading of the text. Students can reread the text to check answers. The second comprehension exercise, *Looking for Details,* concentrates on developing skimming and scanning skills.

5. **Discussion:** Working in small or large groups, students are encouraged to interact with one another to discuss questions that arise from the reading. The discussion questions ask students to relate their experiences to what they have learned from the reading.

6. **Writing skills:** Following each of the sixteen readings, a different aspect of writing at the paragraph level is presented. These aspects include writing topic and supporting sentences, capitalization and punctuation, and using transitions. Exercises on the points taught provide reinforcement.

7. **Writing practice:** Students are asked to write a paragraph, using the ideas they have generated in the discussion section and the grammar points they have practiced. The text takes them through the writing process one step at a time. First they write sentences about themselves, in answer to questions presented in the text. Then they develop an outline. Next students rewrite the sentences from their outline in the form of a paragraph, using a checklist (on their own or with a partner) to check their paragraphs and then making any necessary alterations. Teachers are encouraged to add to the checklist provided any further points they consider important. In the fifth step, students are encouraged to work with a partner or their teacher to correct spelling, punctuation, vocabulary, and grammar. Finally, students prepare the final version of their paragraphs.

Optional Expansion Activities

1. **Quiz:** At the end of each unit is a fun quiz related to the theme of the unit. The answers appear at the end of the book. The quiz questions are meant to be a light-hearted way to end the unit. Use them as a team competition or as a game. Students can also make up further quiz questions to test each other.

2. **Video activity:** Following the quiz is a video activity related to the CNN videotapes that accompany this series. The video activity can be used to expand vocabulary and themes in the unit. Each video

activity ends with a discussion question, which can be used as a springboard for further writing.

3. **Internet activity:** Also at the end of each unit is an Internet activity, which gives students the opportunity to develop their Internet research skills. This activity may be done in a classroom setting, under the guidance of the teacher, or—if students have Internet access—as a homework task leading to a classroom presentation or discussion. Each Internet activity has two parts. The first part involves doing some research on the Internet using the key words suggested. The second part involves evaluating web sites in order to assess the reliability of the information they contain.

Journal Writing

In addition to doing the projects and exercises in the book, I strongly recommend that students be instructed to keep a journal in which they correspond with you. The purpose of this journal is for them to tell you how they feel about the class each day. It gives them an opportunity to tell you what they like, what they dislike, what they understand, and what they don't understand. By having students explain what they have learned in the class, you can discover whether they understand the concepts taught.

Journal writing is effective for two major reasons. First, because this type of writing focuses on fluency and personal expression, students always have something to write about. Second, journal writing can be used to identify language concerns and trouble spots that need further review. In its finest form, journal writing becomes an active dialogue between teacher and student that permits you to learn more about your students' lives and to individualize their language instruction.

References

Blanton, Linda Lonon. 1992. "Reading, Writing, and Authority: Issues in Developmental ESL." *College ESL,* 2, 11–19.

Kroll, Barbara. 1993. "Teaching Writing *Is* Teaching Reading: Training the New Teacher of ESL Composition." In *Reading in the Composition Classroom.* Boston: Heinle & Heinle Publishers, pp. 61–81.

To the Student

This book will teach you to read and write in English. You will study readings on selected themes and learn strategies for writing good sentences on those themes. In the process, you will learn to express your own ideas in sentences and work toward writing a paragraph in good English.

It is important for you to know that writing well in English may be quite different from writing well in your native language. Good Chinese, Arabic, or Spanish writing is different from good English writing. Not only are the styles different, but the organization is different too.

The processes of reading and writing are closely interconnected. Therefore, in this book, we are weaving reading and writing together. I hope that the readings in the book will stimulate your interest to write and that *Weaving It Together* will make writing in English much easier for you.

Note for the New Edition

In this new edition of *Weaving It Together, Book 2*, the readings are longer, and I have added extra vocabulary exercises. There is a new unit with readings from literature. For those of you who enjoy using different media, I have also added CNN video and Internet activities. I hope that you will enjoy using these new features and that *Weaving It Together* will continue to help you toward success.

Your Personality

CHAPTER ONE

Right Brain or Left Brain?

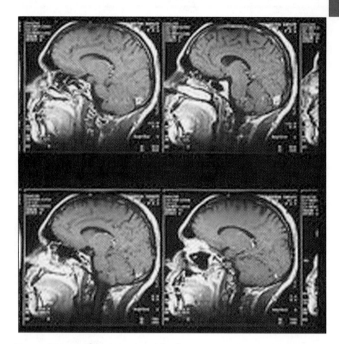

Pre-Reading Activity

Discuss these questions.

1. Do you know the names of the people in the picture on page 1?
2. What are they famous for?
3. All of them are the same in one way. What do you think it is?

Key Vocabulary

Do you know these words? Match the words with the meanings.

1. ⎯⎯ in common
2. ⎯⎯ population
3. ⎯⎯ logic
4. ⎯⎯ have things in order
5. ⎯⎯ punctual
6. ⎯⎯ recognize
7. ⎯⎯ exceptions
8. ⎯⎯ message

a. instruction or news sent to someone or something
b. have things in their right place
c. the same
d. number of people who live in a place
e. remember having heard or seen before
f. thinking that follows rules
g. on time; not late
h. people or things that do not belong with the others

Right Brain or Left Brain?

What do Leonardo da Vinci, Paul McCartney, and Julia Roberts have **in common?** They are all left-handed. Today about 15 percent of the **population** is left-handed. But why are people left-handed? The answer may be in the way the brain works.

Our brain is like a **message** center. Each second, the brain receives more than a million messages from our body and knows what to do with them. People think that the weight of the brain tells how intelligent you are, but this isn't true. Albert Einstein's brain weighed 1,375 grams, but less intelligent people may have heavier brains. What is important is the quality of the brain. The brain has two halves— the right brain and the left brain. Each half is about the same size. The right half controls the left side of the body, and the left half controls the right side of the body. One half is usually stronger than the other. One half of the brain becomes stronger when you are a child and usually stays the stronger half for the rest of your life.

The left side of the brain controls the right side of the body, so when the left brain is stronger, the right hand will be strong and the person may be right-handed. The left half controls speaking, so a person with a strong left brain may become a good speaker, professor, lawyer, or salesperson. A person with a strong left brain may have a strong idea of time and will probably be **punctual.** The person may be strong in math and **logic** and may like to **have things in order.** He or she may remember people's names and like to plan things ahead. He or she may be practical and safe. If something happens to the left side of the brain, the person may have problems speaking and may not know what day it is. The right side of his or her body will become weak.

When the right side of the brain is stronger, the person will have a strong left hand and may be left-handed. The person may prefer art, music, and literature. The person may become an artist, a writer, an inventor, a film director, or a photographer. The person may **recognize** faces, but not remember names. The person may not love numbers or business. The person may like to use his or her feelings, and not look at logic and what is practical. If there is an accident to the right side of the brain, the person may not know where he or she is and may not be able to do simple hand movements.

This does not mean that all artists are left-handed and all accountants are right-handed. There are many **exceptions**. Some right-handers have a strong right brain, and some left-handers have a strong left brain. The best thing would be to use both right and left sides of the brain. There are people who learn to do two things at the same time. They can answer practical questions on the telephone (which uses the left brain) and at the same time play the piano (which uses the right brain), but this is not easy to do!

Vocabulary

Meaning

Complete the sentences with the following words.

punctual	recognize
have things in order	exceptions
logic	population
in common	message

1. Leonardo da Vinci and Julia Roberts have something _____. They are both left-handed.

2. About 15 percent of the _____ is left-handed.

3. Each part of our body sends a _____ to the brain.

4. Right-handed people may not do something because they feel like it. They may do it because there is _____ to it.

5. A right-handed person may like to be neat and _____.

6. A left-handed person may look at a face and _____ the person.

7. A right-handed person doesn't like to be late. He or she is _____.

8. We cannot say that all right-handers have strong left brains and all left-handers have strong right brains. There are _____.

Vocabulary Activity

Answer the questions. Use complete sentences.

1. What do you and your classmates have in common?

   _____

   _____

2. Do you like to have things in order? Give an example.

   _____

   _____

3. Do you know someone who is always punctual?

   _____

   _____

4. What is the population of your country?

   _____

   _____

5. How do you recognize a person from a distance?

   _____

   _____

6. How do you usually leave a message for someone?

   _____

   _____

7. What is an exception to a rule in English grammar or spelling?

   _____

   _____

Comprehension

Looking for the Main Ideas

Read the passage again and look for the MAIN IDEAS. Circle the letter of the best answer.

1. People are right-handed or left-handed because of _____.

    a. the population
    b. the way the brain works
    c. Paul McCartney and Julia Roberts
    d. the messages the brain receives

2. The brain _____.

    a. has two halves
    b. has two left halves
    c. is heavier in intelligent people
    d. is lighter in intelligent people

3. Each side of the brain _____.

    a. likes language and math
    b. controls the same things
    c. controls different things
    d. changes all the time

Looking for Details

Read the passage again and look for DETAILS. Circle T if the sentence is true. Circle F if the sentence is false.

1. Fifty percent of the population is left-handed.   T   F

2. The weight of the brain does not tell how intelligent you are.   T   F

3. A right-handed person may prefer music and art.   T   F

4. A person with a strong right brain may be good at recognizing faces.   T   F

5. Some people can use both sides of the brain at the same time.   T   F

6. A person with a strong right brain may not be practical.   T   F

Discussion

Discuss these questions with your classmates.

1. Do you think children should be forced to be right-handed?

2. Does the word *left* have a negative meaning in your language? Is it bad to be left-handed in your country?

3. Ask a left-handed person these questions:

   - Are your parents left-handed?
   - Are you left-footed?
   - When you play tennis or other sports, do you use your left hand or your right hand?
   - When you were a child, did people try to make you right-handed?
   - Do you want to be right-handed?
   - What things do you find difficult to use (for example, scissors, can openers)?
   - Do you think you write slower than a right-handed person?

In groups, discuss the answers you get.

		Yumi Ono
		3/3/93
		ESL 163
	Left-handed People	Center the title.
Indent the first line.	Left-handed people have many problems living in a world for	
Capitalize the first word in each sentence.	right-handed people. First, driving a car may be a problem. All	
One-inch margin	the important things in the car are on the right. For example,	One-inch margin
	the ignition switch, the gear shift, the accelerator, and the	
	brake are all on the right. Second, using a computer may be a	
	problem. Computers are again made for right-handed people,	
	and all the important keys are on the right. These include the	
	delete key, the enter key, the period, the comma, and other	
	important punctuation marks. In conclusion, left-handed people	
	have to work harder than right-handed people to do simple	
	things.	

Organizing

Paragraph Form

In this book, you will learn how to write a good paragraph. Before you start to write, it is important for you to know the requirements of good paragraph form.

Instructions on Paragraph Form

1. Use lined paper.
2. Write your name, the date, and the course number in the upper right-hand corner of the paper.
3. Write a title in the center at the top of the page.
4. Leave a one-inch margin on both sides of the page.
5. Indent the first line of every paragraph. When you write by hand, indent the first line about one inch from the margin. When you type, indent the first line five spaces. In business letters, you do not have to indent the first line of every paragraph.
6. Write on every other line of the paper.
7. Capitalize the first word in each sentence and end each sentence with a period.

Punctuation and Capitalization

A sentence always begins with a capital letter and ends with a period (.), an exclamation point (!), or a question mark (?). The first word after a comma (,) begins with a small letter. Here are some rules for using capital letters.

Capitalization Rules

1. Capitalize the first word in a sentence.
   Today, about 15 percent of the population is left-handed.
2. Capitalize the pronoun *I*.
   Paul and I are left-handed.

3. Capitalize all proper nouns. Here are some proper nouns:

   a. Names of people and their titles:

      John McEnroe   Mr. John Smith
      Napoleon   Dr. Mary Roberts
      Marilyn Monroe

   b. Names of places you can find on a map:

      Verdugo Road   Times Square
      Central Avenue   Canada
      Lake Victoria   London, England

   c. Names of nationalities, races, languages, and religions:

      American   Hispanic
      Asian   Muslim
      Catholic   Arab

   d. Names of specific organizations (schools, businesses):

      University of California   Glendale College
      Bank of America   Safeway
      International Students Club   Red Cross

   e. Names of school subjects with course numbers:

      English 101   Spanish 01A

   f. Names of days, months, and special days:

      Monday   Independence Day
      May   Halloween

   g. Names of special buildings and bridges:

      White House   Golden Gate Bridge

Exercise 1

Change the small letters to capital letters where necessary.

1. st. mary's college is located in boston, massachusetts.

2. in august 1959, hawaii became the fiftieth state of the united states.

3. I parked my car on the corner of greenwood avenue and lexington.

4. maria is a student from peru. she speaks spanish, french, and italian.

5. there are no classes during christmas, easter, and thanksgiving vacations.

6. students who are buddhist, muslim, christian, and jewish all got together to help.

7. I am taking three classes this semester: english 120, spanish 1A, and business administration.

8. have you been to see the white house in washington, d.c.?

Find the mistakes. There are 10 mistakes in grammar, punctuation, and capitalization. Find and correct them.

There are more than 500 million left-handed people in the world. There are also many left-handers who are famous. Recent american president who are left-handed are Ronald Reagan, george Bush and bill Clinton. Actors such as tom Cruise and robert De Niro and women like queen Elizabeth II and nicole Kidman are also left-handed. In the old days, people thought left-handed people were bad. In japan a long time ago, a man could ask for a divorce if he found that his wife was left-handed. Today, it's not bad to be left-handed.

Answer the following questions. Use capital letters where necessary.

1. What is your full name?

_____

2. Write the names of three other students in your class.

_____

_____

_____

3. What languages do you speak?

_____

4. Write the names of three other languages that students in your class speak.

_____

5. Where do you come from (city and country)?

_____

6. Write the names of five holidays that you know (in the United States or your country).

_____

_____

_____

_____

_____

7. Write the name and address of your school or college.

_____

_____

_____

8. What classes are you going to take this year?

_____

_____

_____

_____

How to Write a Title

A title tells the reader the topic of the paragraph. A title is usually a word or phrase. If it is a sentence, it should not be a long sentence.

Remember these points:

1. Capitalize the first word, last word, and all important words in the title. Do not capitalize prepositions and articles.
   Exception: Capitalize an article that begins the title.

2. Do not underline the title.

3. Do not use a period (.), a comma (,), or quotations marks (" "). But you can use an exclamation mark (!) or a question mark (?).

Examples of titles:

Stronger Right or Left Brain?
The Importance of Having a Friend
My First Day in the United States
Learning Can Be Fun, Too!

Exercise 4

Say what is wrong with the titles below. Then write the titles in the correct way.

1. Eating In The United States Of America.

   _____

   _____

2. "Learning english Is Important."

   _____

   _____

3. I have many problems because I am living away from my family.

   _____

   _____

4. the Most Important Day Of My Life

   _____

   _____

Do You Have a Stronger Left Brain or Right Brain?

This simple writing test will tell you.

1. Write your name on a piece of paper.

2. Did your pen point away from you when you wrote? Was your hand below the line of writing (straight writing)?

3. Did the pen point toward you? Was your hand above the line of writing (hooked writing)?

You have a stronger right brain if

. . . you write straight with your left hand. (See picture 1.)

. . . you write hooked with your right hand. (See picture 2.)

You have a stronger left brain if

. . . you write straight with your right hand. (See picture 3.)

. . . you write hooked with your left hand. (See picture 4.)

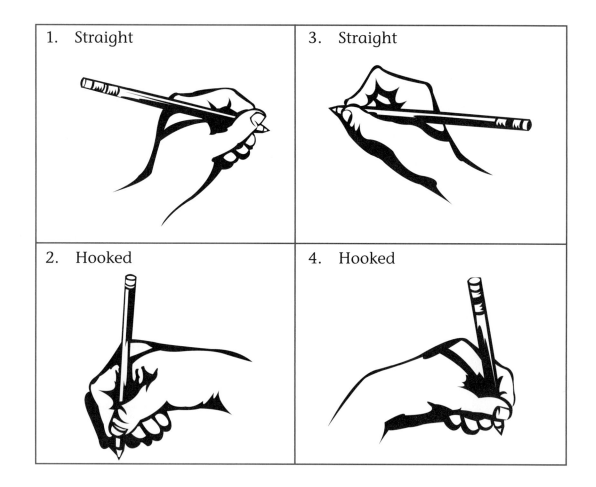

1. Straight

3. Straight

2. Hooked

4. Hooked

CHAPTER TWO

The Shape of the Face

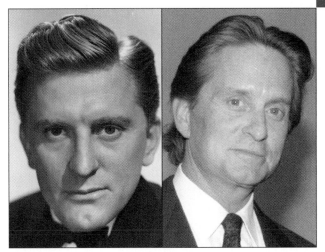

Kirk Douglas   Michael Douglas

Pre-Reading Activity

Discuss these questions.

1. How are the faces of the two people in the photos similar?
2. What is the shape of their faces?
3. What different shapes do faces have?
4. Whom do you most look like in your family?

Key Vocabulary

Do you know these words? Match the words with the meanings.

1 ____ jaw	a.	strength of mind to control your actions
2. ____ cheekbones	b.	easily broken
3. ____ confident	c.	willing to give
4. ____ will	d.	showing artistic ability
5. ____ creative	e.	having a strong belief in your ability
6. ____ generous	f.	the bones below and beside the eyes
7. ____ fragile	g.	the bony parts of the face that hold the teeth

The Shape of the Face

Some people believe that the shape of a person's face shows the general character of the person. The Chinese believe that there are eight basic shapes of the face, and each shape shows a special character. The shapes are round, diamond, rectangle, square, triangle, narrow forehead and wide **jaw,** wide forehead and square chin, and wide forehead and high **cheekbones.** Here is what people say about these shapes.

Round faces have high and flat cheekbones, flat ears, wide noses, and strong mouths with thin lips. People with round faces are very intelligent, and they prefer to work with their brain instead of their body. People with round faces are **confident** and usually live a long life.

Many movie stars and famous women have diamond faces. The diamond face is narrow at the top and has a pointed chin. The Chinese believe that it is lucky if you meet a man or a woman with a diamond face before you go to an important meeting. People with this type of face are generally lucky in love and in their jobs. They may not be happy when they are young, but they get what they want later in their lives. People with diamond faces are warm, but they have a strong **will.**

People with rectangular faces control their feelings, but they are intelligent and **creative.** These people work hard and are very reliable. Their work is very important to them and comes before everything else, even family. They are not easy to be around when they do not feel free or when they feel bored. Many people with rectangular faces are at their best when they are older.

Square faces usually belong to men, but women can also have them. Men with this kind of face are good at making decisions and keeping to them. They are **generous** and honest. They put their friends first in everything. Both men and women with square faces are lucky and live a long life.

A wide forehead, high cheekbones, and a pointed chin make a triangular face. People with triangular faces are lively and intelligent and often stand out from others; however, they worry too much and their emotions are **fragile,** so they can get depressed easily. Because of this, they do better in jobs where they work with people.

The Chinese believe that a person with a wide jaw and narrow forehead is like the earth and changes little. People with this kind of face love success and will almost always get what they want, especially money and all that it brings. A man with this kind of face will not be close to his children, but his children will respect his strength. A woman with this kind of face was Jacqueline Kennedy, who had a strong character even in difficult times.

People with wide foreheads and square chins are intelligent and work hard to get what they want. They can be calm and quiet, or they can be the opposite, too, because they like to get attention. Famous movie people like Paul Newman and Jane Fonda have this kind of face; so did Picasso, the painter. They usually have a long life and save their energy for important times in life.

People with wide foreheads and high cheekbones show strong character and a lot of energy. This helps them to be normal again if something bad happens. They know what they like and don't like to change their habits. Nevertheless, they like to live a full life.

Vocabulary

Meaning

Complete the sentences with the following words.

will	confident
fragile	generous
creative	cheekbones
jaw	

1. Some people have a wide————, which makes their face look wide.

2. Women with high ———— look attractive.

3. People with a strong ———— are able to do what they have to do.

4. Artists are ———— people.

5. People with ———— emotions can get hurt very easily.

6. People with square faces are ———— with their time and money.

7. People with round faces are _____ and walk with their heads held up high.

Vocabulary Activity

Answer the questions. Use complete sentences.

1. Who in the class has a big jaw?

   _____

   _____

2. Who in the class has high cheekbones?

   _____

   _____

3. Who is a creative person you know?

   _____

   _____

4. When are you generous with money?

   _____

   _____

5. What are some objects in a house that are fragile?

   _____

   _____

Comprehension

Looking for the Main Ideas

Circle the letter of the best answer.

1. The Chinese believe that the shape of the face _____.
   a. is not important
   b. can show the character of a person
   c. is important when you want to be a movie star
   d. can show that a person has medical problems

2. The Chinese believe that there are _____.
   a. eight basic shapes of faces
   b. square faces and round faces only
   c. some good shapes and some bad shapes
   d. four basic shapes of faces

3. The Chinese believe that the shape of your face can show _____.
   a. when accidents will happen to you
   b. if you are intelligent
   c. if you are Chinese
   d. if you will have children

Looking for Details

Circle T if the sentence is true. Circle F if the sentence is false.

1. The Chinese believe that it is lucky to meet a person with a diamond face.   T   F

2. Jacqueline Kennedy had a square face.   T   F

3. The Chinese believe that round faces are intelligent.   T   F

4. Jane Fonda has a rectangular face.   T   F

5. The Chinese believe that people with triangular faces can get depressed easily. T   F

6. The Chinese believe that people with diamond faces are not lucky in love. T   F

Discussion

Discuss these questions with your classmates.

1. Do you think there is any truth in reading people's faces (physiognomy)? How reliable is it?

2. Ask the students in your class which part of the face helps them understand a person's character. Fill out the questionnaire below.

3. Discuss what shapes of face, eyes, mouth, ears, etc., show good character.

Name	Country	Shape of Face	Shape of Eyes	Shape of Mouth	Shape of Ears	Other

Organizing

Joining Compound Sentences with *and, but,* or *or*

A *compound sentence* is made by joining two simple sentences. These two simple sentences are joined by a *coordinating conjunction.* In this chapter, we will look at the coordinating conjunctions **and, but,** and **or.**

Using *and* To Join Two Sentences

We can use **and** to join two sentences that are alike or to join to a sentence another sentence that gives extra information.

Examples:

The Chinese believe that there are eight basic shapes of faces. Each shape shows a special character.

The Chinese believe that there are eight basic shapes of faces, **and** each shape shows a special character.

Note: Use a comma before **and.**

Using *but* To Join Two Sentences

We can use **but** to join two sentences that give opposite information or to join a positive sentence and a negative sentence that talk about the same subject:

+, but –
–, but +

Examples:

People with diamond faces may not be happy when they are young. They get what they want later in their lives.

People with diamond faces may not be happy when they are young, **but** they get what they want later in their lives.

Note: Use a comma before **but.**

Using *or* To Join Two Sentences

We can use **or** to join two sentences that give a choice or alternative.

Examples:

People with wide foreheads and square chins can be calm and quiet. They can be just the opposite, too.

People with wide foreheads and square chins can be calm and quiet, **or** they can be just the opposite, too.

Note: Use a comma before **or.**

We only use a comma with **and, but,** or **or** in compound sentences. When we use **and, but,** or **or** in a simple sentence, we do not use a comma. In a sentence, **and, but,** or **or** can join two nouns, two adjectives, two adverbs, or two verbs.

Examples:

1. Two nouns joined by **and**

   Both <u>men</u> and <u>women</u> with square faces are lucky.
         (Noun)   (Noun)

2. Two adjectives joined by **and**

   They are <u>intelligent</u> and <u>creative</u>.
         (Adjective)   (Adjective)

3. Two nouns joined by **or**

   A face may look round because of a small <u>forehead</u> or <u>chin</u>.
                    (Noun)   (Noun)

4. Two adjectives joined by **or**

   They are not easy to be around when they feel
   <u>bored</u> or <u>not free</u>.
   Adjective)   (Adjective)

Compare the sentences you just read with the compound sentences you have studied. Now underline all the coordinating conjunctions (**and, but,** and **or**)in the reading passage. Notice the punctuation with simple and compound sentences.

Use the conjunction in parentheses to join the two sentences into a compound sentence. Use the correct punctuation.

1. Almost all the Chinese emperors had round faces. Many famous explorers had them, too. (and)

    Example: Almost all the Chinese emperors had round faces, and many famous explorers had them, too.

2. People with triangular faces may not be tall. They look tall because of the shape of their body. (but)

    _____

    _____

3. These people are confident. They will usually live a long life. (and)

    _____

    _____

4. Some may be movie stars. They may work as flight attendants. (or)

    _____

    _____

5. People with high cheekbones know what they want. It is hard to make them change their minds. (and)

    _____

    _____

6. People with this shape of face may often be leaders. They may also be criminals. (but)

    _____

    _____

7. They can control their feelings. They are intelligent and creative. (but)

_____

_____

8. Square faces usually belong to men. Women can have them, too. (but)

_____

_____

Exercise 2

Write compound sentences with **and, but,** or **or.** First think of two complete sentences. Then join them with **and, but,** or **or.** Do not forget to punctuate.

1. Write a compound sentence about a characteristic of a person's face. Use the word **and** to join the parts of your compound sentence.

   Example: <u>My grandfather has big ears with big ear lobes, and everybody says he will live for a long time.</u>

   _____

   _____

2. Write a compound sentence about a person's face. Use the word **but.**

   Example: <u>Uncle Joe has a red face, but he does not have a bad temper.</u>

   _____

   _____

3. Write a compound sentence about a person's face. Use the word **or.**

   Example: <u>Tony looks pale, or he may be just tired.</u>

   _____

   _____

Find the mistakes. There are 10 mistakes in grammar, punctuation, and capitalization. Find and correct them.

People with a wide forehead, and high cheekbones have a face that looks solid, and bony. Famous example of people with this face are christopher columbus, greta garbo and ludwig beethoven.

Writing Practice

Here, you will rewrite a paragraph following the rules you have learned in this unit. In Unit Two, you will be writing your own paragraphs.

Work alone or with a friend. The paragraph below has some mistakes. Rewrite the paragraph. Make sure you do these things.

1. Write a title.
2. Indent the first line.
3. Join the sentences with the correct word from the parentheses.
4. Check for capital letters, periods, and commas.

eyes are a very important part of the Face. Your eyes will tell people your real feelings. When a person smiles, check his or her eyes for smile lines (and/but) a warm expression. The lips can lie in a smile (but/and/or) the eyes cannot lie. Your pupils* get bigger or smaller. when you look at the light, they get bigger (but/and) when you look at the dark they get smaller. your pupils also get bigger when you look at something you like (and) they get smaller when you look at something you do not like. So light-colored eyes are easier to read (and/or) dark eyes are a mystery.

Note: The pupil is the small, black, round part in the center of the colored part of your eye.

Write your final copy of the paragraph above.

Do you know these interesting facts about the brain?

Circle T if the sentence is true. Circle F if the sentence is false.

1. Your brain does not feel any pain.   T   F
2. Your brain weighs about one pound.   T   F
3. A woman's brain is heavier than a man's brain.   T   F
4. You are left-handed or right-handed from the day you
   are born.   T   F
5. There are twice as many left-handed men as women.   T   F
6. There have been no left-handed presidents of the United
   States.   T   F
7. The brain works on electricity.   T   F

Video Activity • The Brain and Behavior

1. Before you watch the video, discuss the following.

    a. The doctor in the video is a psychiatrist. What kind of work does this kind of doctor do? What do you think are some things that people can do to keep their brains healthy?

    b. Review the meanings of these important words used in the video: *scan, scrutinize, prescribe, treatment.*

2. Read the following statements. Then, as you watch the video, listen for the information you need to decide whether each one is true or false.

    a. The doctor in the video has scanned 12,000 brains. <u>True</u>

    b. The red areas in the brain images are those that are not active. ____

    c. The brain of the teenaged murderer has decreased brain activity on the left side. ____

    d. Exercise has no effect on people's brains. ____

    e. The main idea of the video is that the new kind of brain imaging scan can help psychiatrists prescribe better treatments for their patients. ____

3. Now mark the statements true or false. The first one is done. Watch the video again if necessary.

4. Do you agree that brain scanning could help to make us happier and more successful?

Internet Activity

What is your star sign? Do you believe in astrology? What does your birthday say about your personality? Find two different web sites that describe your personality based on the date and month of your birth, and compare what they say about you. How much is true?

Food

CHAPTER THREE

Potatoes

Pre-Reading Activity

Discuss these questions.

1. How do you like to eat potatoes?
2. How often do you eat potatoes?
3. What do you eat French fries with?
4. What do you see on the baked potato?
5. Which type of potato do you prefer to eat? Why?

Key Vocabulary

Do you know these words? Match the words with the meanings.

1. ____ imagine
2. ____ instead
3. ____ poison
4. ____ disease
5. ____ advantage
6. ____ baked
7. ____ invented
8. ____ dish

a. a sickness
b. have a picture in your mind about something
c. thought of or made for the first time
d. in place of
e. special cooked food of some kind
f. cooked in the oven
g. something that makes it helpful or useful
h. something that can kill you if you eat or drink it

Potatoes

Can you **imagine** life without French fries? Potatoes are very popular today. They are the fourth most important crop in the world, after wheat, rice, and corn. But in the past, potatoes were not always popular. People in Europe started to eat them only 200 years ago!

In the 1500s, the Spanish went to South America to look for gold. There, they found people eating potatoes. The people of Peru in South America had been eating potatoes for 7,000 years! The Spanish brought the potato back to Europe with them. But people in Europe did not like this strange vegetable. Some people thought that if you ate potatoes, your skin would look like the skin of a potato. Other people could not believe that you ate the underground part of the plant, so they ate the leaves **instead**. This made them sick because there is **poison** in the leaves. Others grew potatoes for their flowers. At one time in France, potato flowers were one of the most expensive flowers. Marie Antoinette, the wife of King Louis XV, wore potato flowers in her hair.

Around 1780, the people of Ireland started to eat potatoes. They found that potatoes had many **advantages.** The potato grew on poor land, and it grew well in their cold and rainy climate. It gave more food than any other plant, and it needed little work. All they had to do was to plant the potatoes, and then they could do other work on the farm. On a small piece of land, a farmer could grow enough potatoes to feed his family. A person could eat 8 to 10 pounds of potatoes a day, with some milk or cheese, and be very healthy. Soon, potatoes became the main food in Ireland. Then, in 1845, a **disease** killed all the potatoes in Ireland. Two million people died of hunger. Many Irish who did not die came to the United States at this time. Over a million Irish came to America; one of them was the great-grandfather of John F. Kennedy.

In other parts of Europe, people did not want to change their old food habits. Some preferred to die of hunger rather than eat potatoes. In 1774, King Frederick of Germany wanted to stop his people from dying of hunger. He understood that potatoes were a good food, so he told the people to plant and eat potatoes or else his men would cut off their noses. The people were not happy, but they had no choice and so started to eat potatoes. Today, people in this part of Germany eat more potatoes than any other nationality. Each person eats about 370 pounds of potatoes every year!

Today, many countries have their own potato **dishes.** Germans eat potato salad, and the United States has the **baked** potato. And, of course, the French **invented** French fries. Now French fries are popular all over the world. The English eat them with salt and vinegar, the French eat them with salt and pepper, the Belgians eat them with mayonnaise, and the Americans eat them with ketchup.

Vocabulary

Meaning

Complete the sentences with the following words.

dishes	invented
poison	advantage
baked	instead
imagine	disease

1. We cannot _____ eating a hamburger without French fries.

2. Some plants have _____ in them and can kill you if you eat them.

3. People didn't grow potatoes for food; they grew them for their flowers _____.

4. The potato got a _____, which killed the plants.

5. Americans cook the potato with its skin in the oven. They call it a _____ potato.

6. From the name, we know that the French _____ French fries.

7. There are many _____ you can make with potatoes.

8. The potato has one big _____ over other crops—it is easy to grow.

Comprehension

Looking for the Main Ideas

Circle the letter of the best answer.

1. Potatoes are _____.
   a. popular today
   b. not popular today
   c. popular only in America
   d. popular only in Europe

2. In the 1500s, people in Europe _____.
   a. liked the potato
   b. had bad skin
   c. did not like the potato as food
   d. invented French fries

3. In about 1780, people started to _____.
   a. eat potatoes in Ireland
   b. grow potatoes for their flowers
   c. go to Peru
   d. die of hunger in America

4. French fries are _____.
   a. a special dish in Belgium
   b. popular all over the world
   c. from Germany
   d. most popular in America

Looking for Details

One word in each sentence is not correct. Rewrite the sentence with the correct word.

1. Potatoes grew in Europe 7,000 years ago.

   _____

   _____

2. In the 1700s, the Spanish brought the potato back to Europe.

   _____

   _____

3.	There is poison in the skin of the potato.

_____

_____

4.	A disease killed the people in Ireland in 1845.

_____

_____

5.	Five million people died of hunger in Ireland.

_____

_____

6.	The potato dish of Germany is the baked potato.

_____

_____

7.	The Americans invented French fries.

_____

_____

Discussion

1.	Find out from the students in your class about the main food and drink in their country. Fill out the questionnaire below.

Name	Country	Main Food	Main Drink
Berta	Mexico	Tortillas	Coffee

2.	Is the main drink in your country good for you? Why or why not?

3.	In your country, are there any customs related to the main food?

Now read the following paragraph written by a student. Can you guess where the student is from?

Model Paragraph

Bread

In my country, bread is an important part of our everyday food. When we sit down for a meal, there is always bread on the table. For breakfast, we have bread with butter or cheese. Some people have jam or olives. For lunch, we have bread with a meat or vegetable dish. Poor people eat more bread with a small piece of meat or vegetable or cheese. For example, the lunch of a worker may be a loaf of bread with some yogurt. Again at dinner, we eat bread with whatever food there is on the table. When there is rice, we have bread, too. We think that if there is no bread, there is no food.

Organizing

The Topic Sentence

Underline the first sentence in the model paragraph above. It is the topic sentence.

The *topic sentence* is the most important sentence in a paragraph. It tells the reader what the paragraph is about, or its main idea. The topic sentence is usually the first sentence in a paragraph. The topic sentence has two parts: the topic and the controlling idea. The *topic* is the subject of your paragraph. It is what you are writing about.

Example:

Bread is an important part of our everyday food.

Topic: Bread

Circle the topic in these sentences.

1. Potatoes are good for you.

2. There are many kinds of rice.

3. The hamburger is a popular food in America.

4. People all around the world drink tea.

5. Bread is the poor man's food.

The *controlling idea* limits or controls your topic to the one aspect that you want to write about.

Example:

Rice   plays   an important part in some ceremonies.
(Topic)   (Controlling idea)
or
Rice   is   a nutritious part of our diet.
(Topic)   (Controlling idea)

A topic can have more than one controlling idea. You could write one paragraph about how rice plays an important part in some ceremonies, a second paragraph about how rice is a nutritious part of our diet, and a third paragraph about another aspect of rice. There are many possibilities.

Exercise 2

Underline the controlling idea in these topic sentences.
1. Bread is an important part of our diet.
2. Bread plays an important part in our religion.
3. Potatoes are easy to grow.
4. Potatoes are the basic food of the Irish.
5. French fries are popular all over the world.

Topic sentences are often opinions. A simple fact is not a good topic sentence because there is nothing more you can say about it. If a topic sentence is an opinion, then you can write a paragraph about it.

Exercise 3

Work with a partner. Decide which sentence, a or b, is a fact.

1. a. Rice is a cereal.
    b. In some countries, people eat too much rice.
2. a. The potato is a vegetable.
    b. Potatoes are good for you.
3. a. Rice contains starch.
    b. Rice should be cooked in a special pot.
4. a. Drinking coffee helps you concentrate.
    b. Coffee is made from coffee beans.
5. a. Chewing gum is good for you.
    b. Chewing gum is made from plastic and rubber.
6. a. Coffee contains caffeine.
    b. The best coffee comes from Colombia.

Another kind of topic sentence divides the topic into different parts.

Examples:

(1) Potatoes are good for you in three ways.
(2) There are four basic methods of eating French fries.
(3) Potato-eaters fall into different groups.

When you use this kind of topic sentence, you need to support it by talking about the different parts. For example, to support sentence (1), you would write about the three ways potatoes are good for you.

Put a checkmark (✓) in the blank if the sentence is a good topic sentence.

_____ 1. Bread is made from flour.

_____ 2. Drinking too much coffee may be dangerous for you in several ways.

_____ 3. In some countries, people have very different ideas about drinking tea.

_____ 4. Potatoes are a root vegetable.

_____ 5. Rice is the basic food for half of the world's population.

_____ 6. Potatoes contain many nutrients.

_____ 7. Rice may be cooked in four ways.

Find the mistakes. There 10 mistakes in grammar, capitalization, and spelling. Find and correct them.

The incas in south america grow potatoes for thousands of years before the spanish arrived. The potatoe was the main part of their diet, and culture. The incas measured time by how long it took to cook potatoes. They also used potatoes to tell their Fortune. If they found an odd number of potatoes, it was bad luck. If they found a even number, it was good luck.

Writing Practice

Choose one of the topics below:

1. The basic food in my country
2. The main drink in my country

1. Pre-writing.

Work with a group, a partner, or alone.

a. Write your topic at the top of your paper. (Say what your main food or drink is.)

b. Then ask a question about your topic. This will help you to get ideas. Choose one of these question words:

Who?
What?/In what way?
Where?
When?
Why?

Example:

Rice is an important food in my country.

Question: Why?

c. Write down as many answers as you can. If you find that the question word does not work, try another question word.

2. Develop an outline.

a. Organize your ideas.
Step 1: Write a topic sentence.
Step 2: Choose some of the answers to your question to use as supporting sentences.

b. Make a more detailed outline. The paragraph outline on the next page will help you.

Paragraph Outline

(Topic sentence) _____.

(Supporting fact) _____.

(Supporting fact) _____.

(Supporting fact) _____.

(Concluding sentence) _____.

3. Write a rough draft.

4. Revise your rough draft.

    Using the checklist below, check your rough draft or let your partner check it.

    Paragraph Checklist

    _____ Did you give your paragraph a title?
    _____ Did you indent the first line?
    _____ Did you write on every other line? (Look at pages 8–9 for instructions on paragraph form.)
    _____ Does your paragraph have a topic sentence?
    _____ Does your topic sentence have a controlling idea?
    _____ Do your other sentences support your topic sentence?
    _____ Are your ideas in the correct order?
    _____ Does your paragraph have a concluding sentence?

5. Edit your paragraph.

    Work with a partner or your teacher to edit your paragraph. Check spelling, punctuation, vocabulary, and grammar.

6. Write your final copy.

CHAPTER FOUR

Delicacies

Louise's Restaurant

SALADS

Snake Skin Salad - smoked snake skin slices over green salad with lemon dressing....................7.75

APPETIZERS

Fried Ants - delicious deep-fried ants................................8.95
Fried Brains - delicious fried lamb's brains.......................12.95
Egg Forty Years Old! - a true delicacy.............................95.00

SPECIALTIES

B.B.Q. Snake - cobra served with rice.......................................25.00
Ant and Spider Burgers - a house specialty, with mashed ants and spiders and garlic...............22.50

DESSERTS

Chocolate Ants - ants covered in dark chocolate.....................6.00
Honey-Coated Termites - served with ice cream.......................6.00

Pre-Reading Activity

Discuss these questions.

1. Discuss the items on the menu.
2. Which ones would you want to eat? Why or why not?
3. What item would you like to add to this menu?

Key Vocabulary

Do you know these words? Match the words with the meanings.

1. _____ delicacy
2. _____ alive
3. _____ pork
4. _____ grilled
5. _____ appetizer
6. _____ native
7. _____ dessert
8. _____ paste

a. the last part of a meal, usually a sweet dish
b. original to a land
c. a special food that is expensive or hard to find
d. not dead
e. a soft, smooth cream
f. a small amount of food served before the main meal
g. cooked on metal bars over a fire
h. meat from a pig

Delicacies

Would you like some chicken feet? How about frog's legs? Well, you can't say no to a fifty-year-old egg! It's a **delicacy** that people pay a lot of money for, believe it or not. People in different parts of the world eat just about everything, from elephant's trunks to monkey's brains.

Chicken feet are a favorite **appetizer** in China, while in Taiwan turkey feet are a favorite. In Taiwan, people have both chicken feet and turkey feet in their salads. Whereas Americans like the white meat of a chicken, people in Taiwan prefer other parts of the chicken, like the dark meat and the inside parts. They often deep-fry the skin and serve it separately, along with the main meal.

Snakes and eels are delicacies in most parts of the world. In France and England, fish shops sell eels that are **alive.** In Asia, there are special restaurants for eating snakes. Everything on the menu is snake: snake soup, snake appetizers, snake main course, and snake **desserts!** When you go to the restaurant, the snakes are alive. You choose the snake you want to eat. Then the waiter kills the snake before your very eyes!

People line up in front of restaurants in Malaysia, Singapore, Thailand, and Indonesia to get fish heads. The restaurants prepare the whole fish, but people start by eating the head, which they believe is the tastiest part of the fish. So many people ask for fish heads that the price of fish heads is higher than the price of the best steak.

What about eating a fish that can kill you? The Japanese put their lives in danger every time they eat this delicacy. The fish is called the blowfish, and it is very poisonous. Although they know that they could die, they continue to eat it. Every year, the Japanese eat 20,000 tons of blowfish, and 70 to 100 people die from it every year.

Rats and mice are also a special food in some parts of the world. In China, people like rice rats especially. They clean and salt them and leave them in oil. Then they hang them to dry. These rats sell in the market for twice the price of the best **pork.** Farmers in Thailand and the Philippines also love rice rats. In Vietnam, mice from the rice fields are fried or **grilled.** In Spain, there is a traditional dish called paella, which is made with rice and pieces of fish. In the town of Valencia, this dish also has rat meat to give it a special flavor.

Insects like termites, ants, and bees are delicacies to many people. In Africa, people fight over termite nests. They eat the termites alive and say that they taste like pineapple. In India, people make the ants into a **paste** and eat them with curry. In Borneo, people mix ants with rice. They say that the ants give the rice a special flavor. In Australia, the **native** people drink ants. They mash them in water and say that the drink tastes like lemonade! And bees are delicious when you fry them. You just can't stop eating them!

Vocabulary

Meaning

Complete the sentences with the following words.

native	grilled
delicacy	alive
appetizer	dessert
pork	paste

1. People pay lot of money for a _____ like a fifty-year-old egg.

2. In some fish shops, they sell fish that are not dead but _____.

3. Meat can be _____ over a fire.

4. In Asia, people have pigs for _____.

5. In Asia, snake can be an _____ before the main meal.

6. The _____ people of Australia are the Aborigines.

7. It's nice to have a sweet _____ after the main meal.

8. Sometimes, people make ants into a _____ like a cream.

Vocabulary Activity

Answer the questions. Use complete sentences.

1. What is a favorite appetizer in your country?

   _____

   _____

2. What is your favorite dessert?

   _____

   _____

3. What food do you like grilled?

   _____

   _____

4. What plant or animal is native to your country?

   _____

   _____

5. What kinds of food do people make with pork?

   _____

   _____

6. What food comes in a paste?

   _____

   _____

7. What is a delicacy you like or don't like?

   _____

   _____

Comprehension

Looking for the Main Ideas

Circle the letter of the best answer.

1. People in different parts of the world eat _____ .
   a. only frog's legs
   b. just about everything
   c. only legs, brains, and eggs
   d. mostly insects and snakes

2. In most parts of the world, snakes and eels are _____ .
   a. delicacies
   b. only appetizers
   c. not found in shops or restaurant
   d. desserts

3. Insects are _____ .
   a. good only with lemonade
   b. special in pineapple
   c. delicious to many people
   d. popular in Africa only

Looking for Details

Circle T if the sentence is true. Circle F if the sentence is false.

1. In Asia, there are special restaurants for eating snakes.   T   F

2. In Australia, they mash ants in rice.   T   F

3. In India, people make ants into a soup.   T   F

4. Some people say that bees are delicious when you fry them.   T   F

5. In Africa, people say that ants taste like eels.   T   F

6. Some people pay a lot of money for old eggs.   T   F

Discussion

Discuss these questions with your classmates.

1. Do you know about any other strange foods that people eat?

2. Did you ever eat a kind of food that was strange for you? What was it like?

3. Describe a delicacy that people eat in your country.

Now read the following paragraph written by a student. Can you guess where the student is from?

Model Paragraph

A Specialty in My Country

The people in my country make a special dish from the izote flower, which is delicious to eat. The flower grows on top of a beautiful tree. You can see these trees in gardens of houses. You can also buy izote flowers in the market. The best time for the flower is in the summer, from November to March. From the flowers we make a special dish that we eat almost every week in the summer. To prepare this dish, we boil the petals of the flower in water with salt and garlic. Then we take out the petals and add them to beaten eggs. We fry this mixture like an omelet. When it is ready, we eat it with tomato sauce. The izote flower is a special flower in my country.

Organizing

The first sentence in the model paragraph is the topic sentence. The next sentences are supporting sentences. The last sentence is the concluding sentence.

Supporting Sentences

Supporting sentences tell more about the topic introduced in the topic sentence. Supporting sentences give the reader more facts about or examples of the topic.

Example:

Topic sentence: The people in my country make a special dish from the izote flower.

Supporting sentences: Where the flower grows
Where you can buy the flower
When you can buy the flower
When you eat the dish
How you make it
How you eat it

Exercise 1

Look at the following groups of sentences. The topic sentence is underlined. All except for one of the sentences in each group support the topic sentence. Find the sentence that does not support the topic sentence. Circle the letter of your answer.

1. The carambola is a popular fruit in Taiwan.
   a. It is not expensive.
   b. You can buy it in any supermarket or fruit store in my country.
   c. It is good for you when you are sick.
   d. Most Americans do not like the carambola.

2. The platano, which looks like a banana, has many uses in my country, Peru.
   a. It is an export for my country.
   b. It is used in many kinds of dishes.
   c. Bananas are also a favorite.
   d. It is a supplement for milk.

3. <u>Ginger is a traditional seasoning in China.</u>
   a. It is used in many traditional dishes.
   b. The Chinese have used ginger for a long time.
   c. It is an old custom to use ginger when the dish has a strong smell.
   d. Ginger is expensive in the United States.

4. <u>Soya beans are becoming popular all over the world.</u>
   a. They have always been popular in Asia.
   b. They are easy to grow.
   c. They are not as good as meat.
   d. They have a high food value.

The Concluding Sentence

The last sentence in your paragraph is called the *concluding sentence.* This sentence tells the reader it is the end of the paragraph.

The concluding sentence and the topic sentence are similar. They are both general sentences. You can write the concluding sentence like the topic sentence, but use different words.

Two ways to write a concluding sentence are to

1. Say the topic sentence in different words

   or

2. Summarize the main points in the paragraph.

Many concluding sentences begin with one of these phrases:
In conclusion, ...
In summary, ...

Write a concluding sentence for each of the topic sentences below.

Example:

Topic sentence: Kimchi is an indispensable side dish at meals in Korea.

Concluding sentence: In conclusion, there is no day without kimchi on the table in my country, Korea.

1. In Japan, we use seaweed in many of our traditional meals.

    _____

    _____

2. Americans eat turkey on two of their traditional holidays.

    _____

    _____

3. In many countries, it is usual to eat food with hot peppers.

    _____

    _____

4. Beans play an important part in Brazilian food.

    _____

    _____

5. The French like to eat cheese and have over 300 different cheeses.

    _____

    _____

Find the mistakes. There are 10 mistakes in grammar, punctuation, capitalization, and spelling. Find and correct them.

We all know that muslims don't eat porks but many people don't know that in pakistan they never offer beef to a important guest. Beef is cheap and easily available, so a pakistani would never offer a guest something as common as steak. Instead, he or she would serve leg of lam as an appetize and chicken, or fish as main course or the other way around.

Writing Practice

1. Pre-writing.

    Work with a group, a partner, or alone.
    a. Write the name of a specialty or delicacy in your country (the topic).
    b. Now write a controlling idea about the topic. (Say why it is important/special/traditional.)
    c. Then ask questions about your controlling idea. Use some of the following question words: When? Where? Who? How? Why?

    Example:
    A traditional food in my country is bean sprout soup.
    Questions: When do you eat it?
    How do you make it?
    Why do people eat it?

2. Develop an outline.
    a. Organize your ideas.
    Step 1: Write a topic sentence.
    Step 2: Choose some of the answers to your questions to use as supporting sentences.
    b. Make a more detailed outline. The paragraph outline on the next page will help you.

Paragraph Outline

(Topic sentence) _____.

(Supporting sentence 1) _____.

(Supporting sentence 2) _____.

(Supporting sentence 3) _____.

(Supporting sentence 4) _____.

(Concluding sentence) _____.

3. Write a rough draft.

4. Revise your rough draft.

    Using the checklist below, check your rough draft or let your partner check it.

    Paragraph Checklist
    _____ Did you give your paragraph a title?
    _____ Did you indent the first line?
    _____ Did you write on every other line?
    _____ Does your paragraph have a topic sentence?
    _____ Does your topic sentence have a controlling idea?
    _____ Do your other sentences support your topic sentence?
    _____ Are your ideas in the correct order?
    _____ Does your paragraph have a concluding sentence?

5. Edit your paragraph.

    Work with a partner or your teacher to edit your paragraph. Check spelling, punctuation, vocabulary, and grammar.

6. Write your final copy.

Do you know these interesting facts about food?

Circle T if the sentence is true. Circle F is the sentence is false.

1. The Irish drink more tea than any other people.   T   F
2. American children eat more candy than children of any other nationality.   T   F
3. It is possible to eat a different kind of hamburger every day in the United States for a whole year.   T   F
4. America's favorite fruit is the apple.   T   F
5. The basic food of half of the world's population is rice.   T   F
6. Peanuts grow on small trees.   T   F
7. The ancient Romans ate mice.   T   F
8. Apple pie is America's favorite dessert.   T   F
9. If the pieces are put end to end, one pound of spaghetti will measure 320 feet.   T   F
10. The average American chews twenty-four packs of chewing gum a year.   T   F

Video Activity • Shopping for Healthy Food

1. What are some kinds of food that people should eat to stay healthy? Which foods are the least healthy? Should people go to the grocery store when they are hungry? Why or why not?

2. Circle the correct answer to each of the following questions. Some questions have more than one correct answer.

   a. What does the woman in the video say people should do before shopping for food?

   Exercise   Plan weekly meals   Avoid eating   Make a list

   b. What are "the original fast foods"?

   Fruits   Vegetables   Yogurt   Chips and dip

   c. Breads should be high in

   Sugar   Fiber   Enriched flour   Calories

   d. What kinds of fish are rich in omega-3 fatty acids?

   Tuna and trout   Salmon and shrimp   Tuna and salmon

   e. Healthy dairy products include

   Ice cream   Yogurt   Tofu   Low-fat cheese

3. After you watch the video, check your answers. Discuss which tips from the video could be helpful for your diet.

Internet Activity

What is an unusual food you would like to try? Choose one type of food and go to the Internet to find out more about its history and how it is grown or made. Write a paragraph describing this food to someone who has never heard of it.

Customs and Traditions

CHAPTER FIVE

The Persian New Year

Pre-Reading Activity

Discuss these questions.

1. When do you celebrate the New Year?
2. How do you celebrate the New Year?
3. Most people celebrate the New Year on January 1. When do other people celebrate the New Year?

Key Vocabulary

Do you know these words? Match the words with the meanings.

1. _____ at least
2. _____ pastry
3. _____ symbol
4. _____ pots and pans
5. _____ knock
6. _____ household
7. _____ treats

a. hit something, usually making a noise
b. all the people living together in a house
c. special things that give pleasure, like candies
d. a sign or object that represents a person, thing, or idea
e. not less than, probably more than
f. a sweet mixture of flour, fat, sugar, and water that is baked
g. metal containers used for cooking

The Persian New Year

The celebration of the Persian New Year is a little different from other New Year celebrations. Persia is the old name for Iran. The Persian New Year is called *Nowrooz,* which means "new day." Celebration of Nowrooz started about 3,000 years ago. It is a big family celebration, and people return to their hometowns and villages to celebrate the New Year with their family and friends. Nowrooz begins on the third Wednesday in March, which can be between the dates of March 19 and 22 and is the first day of spring. It lasts for thirteen days.

People start preparing for the celebration weeks ahead of time by cleaning their homes. They wash their rugs and curtains, clean their furniture, and often paint the walls of their home. They also make or buy **at least** one set of new clothes for each person. They bake **pastries** and put seeds in a pot to grow into a green plant as a **symbol** of spring and new birth.

Weeks before Nowrooz, every **household** lays special things on a table to symbolize the holiday season, just as people in the West decorate a Christmas tree. Because seven is a lucky number, there are seven things on the table beginning with the Persian letter *seen* (the English "s"). The seven things on the table are *samam* (a Persian snack made of flour and sugar), *skeh* (a coin), *sabzee* (green vegetables), *sonbol* (a hyacinth flower), *seer* (garlic), *senjeed* (a dried fruit), and *serkeh* (vinegar). Other things are also put on the table, such as apples, sugar, cookies, candles, a mirror, and a bowl with goldfish. They say that if you look at the goldfish as the New Year comes, it will bring good luck.

Many people dress up as Hadji Firooz, who is a symbolic character of the New Year, just as Santa Claus is of Christmas. Hadji Firooz wears a red satin costume and has black makeup on his face. He sings and dances through the streets, telling everyone that the New Year is coming. Today, people see him in shopping malls, just as you can see Santa Claus in the United States or in Britain.

First, on the last Wednesday before Nowrooz, people light fires in public places. This is when the celebration begins. Family members line up and jump over the fire. This is to bring light and happiness throughout the coming year. Children run through the streets. They bang on **pots and pans** with spoons to beat out the last unlucky Wednesday of the year. They **knock** on doors and ask for **treats** like candy, just as children do on Halloween in other countries.

Then, on the night before Nowrooz, the whole family gathers around the table with the seven dishes. The oldest person in the family stands up, gives everyone good wishes, and hands out fresh sweets, pastries, and coins. People spend the first few days of the New Year visiting older family members and other relatives. They give gifts and eat wonderful meals.

Finally, thirteen days after the New Year starts, families leave their houses and go outside to a park or somewhere by a river where it is cool and grassy. They have fun by playing games, singing, and dancing. They also have a wonderful picnic and eat and relax; this ends the Nowrooz celebration until next year.

Vocabulary

Meaning

Complete the sentences with the following words.

symbol	pots and pans	at least	treat
pastries	household	knock	

1. A person buys _____ one piece of new clothing for the New Year.

2. It is usual to eat _____ during the Persian New Year holiday.

3. Candy or chocolate is always a _____ for a child.

4. Children go to a home and _____ on the door to ask for candy.

5. A goldfish in a bowl is a _____ of good luck.

6. During the New Year celebration, each _____ has a table with seven things on it.

7. To make a lot of noise, children bang on _____ with spoons.

Vocabulary Activity

Answer with complete sentences.

1. What is your favorite pastry?

   _____

2. What is the heart a symbol of?

   _____

3. Where do you usually see pots and pans?

   _____

4. When do you knock on a door?

   _____

5. How many people are in your household?

   _____

6. What is your favorite treat?

   _____

Comprehension

Looking for the Main Ideas

Circle the letter of the best answer.

1. Nowrooz _____.
   a. starts on the thirteenth day of spring
   b. celebrates spring
   c. celebrates the New Year
   d. is celebrated differently in every country

2. For the Persian New Year celebration, people _____.
   a. lay seven special things on a table
   b. eat a lot of vegetables
   c. lay seven delicious dishes on a table
   d. have a Christmas tree

3. The celebration starts with _____ .
   a. people visiting relatives
   b. fires burning in public places
   c. a picnic
   d. singing and dancing

Looking for Details

Use complete sentences to answer the questions.

1. When does the Persian New Year begin?

   _____

2. How long does Nowrooz last?

   _____

3. How many things are put on the table to symbolize the New Year?

   _____

4. What color costume does Hadji Firooz wear?

   _____

5. On the night before the New Year, who stands up and gives people pastries and coins?

   _____

6. Where do people go on the thirteenth day?

   _____

Discussion

Discuss these questions with your classmates.
1. Which holiday is the most fun and enjoyable?
2. Do you think we should have more holidays? Why or why not?
3. What is a good time of year to have holidays?

Now read the following paragraph written by a student. Can you guess where the student is from?

Model Paragraph

New Year in My Country

In my country, we call the New Year Tet. First, on the night the New Year begins, we go to the temple. We pray to Buddha, give thanks for the past year, and pray that the new year will be happy. Then we return home. Next, just before midnight, my father bows before an altar we have for our dead relatives. He offers food to the relatives and invites them to join the family. At midnight, we have firecrackers, and children make a lot of noise. It is Tet. The New Year is here. Finally, we sit down and have a big and delicious dinner. We celebrate all night.

Organizing

Describing a Process

When you want to tell about how you do something, like take a bath or wash your car, you must list the main steps. Make sure that the steps are in the correct order. Then to make the order clear to the reader, use the following words, which show time order:

First,$\downarrow$. . . **(Second, . . .   Third, . . .)**
Next,$\downarrow$. . .
Then . . .
Finally/Lastly,$\downarrow$. . .

These words come at the beginning of a sentence. Note that you use a comma (,) after each word except **then.** You do not need to use these words in each sentence of your paragraph.

Now underline the words that show time order in the model paragraph.

Exercise 1

Put the following sentences in the correct order. Number them 1, 2, 3, 4, ...

1.   To wash your hair, follow these steps.
     _____ Put some shampoo on your hair.
     __1__ Wet your hair with water.
     _____ Rinse off the shampoo.
     _____ Lather your hair with shampoo.
     _____ Dry your hair with a towel.
     _____ Repeat the process.

2.   Washing dishes is easy.
     _____ Wash the plates in soapy water with a brush.
     _____ Remove pieces of food from the plates.
     _____ Dry the plates with a towel.
     _____ Rinse off the soapy water.

3.   Cleaning windows is not difficult.
     _____ You need a bucket and a large sponge.
     _____ Dry the windows with a paper towel.
     _____ Wet the sponge, and wipe the windows with it.
     _____ Fill the bucket with water and a little ammonia.
     _____ Your windows will shine.

Punctuation

Comma (,) with Items in a Series

You use a comma to separate three or more items in a series. Do not use a comma if there are only two items.

Examples:

There are other things on the table, such as apples, sugar, cookies, candles, a mirror, and a bowl with goldfish.

They have fun by playing games, singing, and dancing.

Hadji Firooz sings and dances through the streets.
(No comma needed.)

They eat cookies or pastries.
(No comma needed.)

Exercise 2

Put commas in these sentences where necessary. Note that some sentences do not need a comma.

1. The oldest person gives out sweets pastries and coins.

2. The day after the beginning of Nowrooz we visited our grandparents uncle and aunt.

3. Next year Nowrooz starts on March 20 or 21.

4. We see Hadji Firooz in streets or malls.

5. The last day of Nowrooz is fun and exciting.

6. People clean their curtains and furniture.

Find the mistakes. There are 10 mistakes in punctuation, capitalization, and spelling. Find and correct them.

The Chinese New Year celebration is fifteen days long. The Chinese clean their homes and decorate two. They also buy new clothes and prepare plenty of food. The big celebration start on new year's eve. First, they have a big dinner with plenty of food. There are always special foods like a whole fish chicken and long noodles for long life. After dinner, the whole family sits up for the night. They play games, or watch television. Finally there are fireworks all over the sky at midnight.

Writing Practice

Choose one of the topics below:
1. Celebrating New Year
2. Celebrating Christmas or another holiday
3. Preparing a special dinner

1. Pre-writing.

Work with a partner. Tell your partner how you celebrate the New Year (or celebrate another holiday or prepare a special dinner). Then write down what you do first, what you do next, what you do after that, ...

2. Develop an outline.

Number your sentences in the correct order. Then rewrite all the sentences in a paragraph. Use words showing time order. The paragraph outline below will help you.

Paragraph Outline

(Topic sentence) _____ .

First, _____ .

Next, _____ .

Then _____ .

Finally, _____ .

3. Write a rough draft.

4. Revise your rough draft.

> Using the checklist below, check your rough draft or let your partner check it.

Paragraph Checklist

_____ Did you give your paragraph a title?
_____ Did you indent the first line?
_____ Did you write on every other line? (Look at pages 8–9 for instructions on paragraph form.)
_____ Does your paragraph have a topic sentence?
_____ Are your ideas in the correct order?
_____ Does your paragraph have a concluding sentence?

5. Edit your paragraph.

> Work with a partner or your teacher to edit your paragraph. Check spelling, punctuation, vocabulary, and grammar.

6. Write your final copy.

CHAPTER SIX

Celebrating Fifteen

Pre-Reading Activity

Discuss these questions.

1. What is the girl in the photo wearing? Why?

2. What is a special birthday for a young person in your country? What does it mean?

3. How do people usually celebrate it?

Key Vocabulary

Do you know these words? Match the words with the meanings.

1. _____ afford
2. _____ bouquet
3. _____ proud of
4. _____ pose
5. _____ godparents
6. _____ blessing

a. pleased because of something the person has done

b. adults who are close family friends and guide you through your life

c. ask for God's help and protection for someone or something

d. a bunch of flowers

e. hold yourself still for a photograph

f. have enough money for

Celebrating Fifteen

A quincenera (pronounced "kin-sin-yera") is a special celebration held for many girls in Spanish-speaking communities of the United States and in Latin America on their fifteenth birthday. The celebration may be different in different countries. The word *quincenera* can refer to the celebration or to the girl. This birthday is special because it celebrates that a girl is not a child anymore and has become a woman. It is a very important day for many young girls, a day they dream about for a long time. Everyone who knows the girl will celebrate it with a church ceremony and a big party.

There is a lot of preparation before a quincenera celebration. The most important and expensive thing is the girl's dress. The dress is like a bride's dress but is usually pink; however, today many girls wear dresses in other light colors, also. The birthday girl chooses fourteen girls and fourteen boys who will be her attendants at the ceremony and the dinner dance that follows. Traditionally, these girls and boys are younger than the birthday girl, but sometimes they are the same age. The dresses for the girls must be in the same color and style, just as the suits for the boys are in the same color and style. The reason for this is that all eyes will go to the birthday girl on that special day. Then the family orders a cake that is special like a wedding cake. Sometimes the **godparents** pay for it. Many times, the cake is so big that it needs a special table. Next, the parents rent a hall for the party and rent a band to play music. After that, they decide on the special food to serve the guests. Often a quincenera celebration can cost as much as a big wedding; the size of the party depends on how much the girl's parents can **afford.**

On the night before the girl's fifteenth birthday, a band plays in the evening outside her window. Then the day of her birthday arrives. First, the girl's family, her godparents, and her attendants go to a religious ceremony in the church. The girl receives a **bouquet** of flowers and **blessings** and prayers that will help her to live a strong life. Her parents are **proud of** their grown-up daughter, and they embrace her. Then she leaves the church with her attendants and goes to the hall for the special party. Before they go to the party, they **pose** for photographs.

The hall is beautifully decorated with flowers, and it is full of guests. They wait for the girl and her family to arrive. The band plays music, and the party begins with a dinner. After the dinner, the girl dances the first dance with her father. Then the other attendants start to dance, followed by the guests. Everyone has a good time, and they all dance until midnight. It is a day she will always remember.

Vocabulary

Meaning

Complete the sentences with the following words.

bouquet	afford
godparents	proud of
pose	blessings

1. A quincenera is expensive, and many parents cannot _____ to have one for their daughter.

2. The girl's _____ help her with guidance and advice throughout her life.

3. The quincenera holds a _____ in the church.

4. In the church, the girl receives prayers and _____.

5. When the ceremony ends, the parents are _____ their daughter.

6. The quincenera and her attendants _____ for photos with which to remember this special day.

Vocabulary Activity

Answer the questions. Use complete sentences.

1. Who gives you guidance in your life—your godparents or someone else?

_____

2. When do you give a bouquet of flowers?

   _____

3. What can you not afford to buy right now?

   _____

4. What are you proud of about yourself?

   _____

5. When do you pose for a photograph?

   _____

6. Where can you receive a blessing?

   _____

Comprehension

Looking for the Main Ideas

Circle the letter of the best answer.

1. A quincenera is _____.
   a. another name for a big birthday party
   b. a fifteenth birthday celebration held for girls in many Latin American countries
   c. the word for "celebration" in Spanish
   d. a special birthday for boys and girls when they are fifteen

2. Before the quincenera, _____.
   a. the girl must make a dress
   b. there is a lot of preparation
   c. the girl asks fourteen boys to dance with her
   d. the girl's parents make a cake

3. On the day of the quincenera, there is _____.
   a. only a church ceremony
   b. a church ceremony, a dinner, and a dance
   c. only a dinner and a dance
   d. a party for the girl's relatives

Looking for Details

Use complete sentences to answer the questions.

1. What is the traditional color for the quincenera's dress?

   _____

2. How many girl and boy attendants does she have?

   _____

3. Where does the girl stand in the church?

   _____

4. What do her godparents give her?

   _____

5. Where does she go with her attendants after the church ceremony?

   _____

6. With whom does the quincenera dance first?

   _____

Discussion

Discuss these questions with your classmates.
1. How do people celebrate a special birthday, a special day for a young person, or a name day in your country?
2. What kind of preparations do they make for this day?
3. Describe a wedding in your country.

Now read the following paragraph written by a student. What country does the student come from?

Model Paragraph

A Wedding in My Country

Last year, my oldest brother got married. His bride was his friend's sister. First, they had a civil marriage in the town hall. A few weeks later, they had a church wedding. The bride wore a beautiful white dress and a veil over her face. The bridegroom wore a tuxedo. After the religious ceremony was over, the newlyweds and the guests went to a restaurant near the church. Here there was a wonderful wedding reception with all kinds of hot and cold food. After that, there was music and dancing. Before the reception ended, the bride and groom met and thanked every guest. Finally, after the reception was over, the newlyweds went on a trip to Hawaii for their honeymoon.

Organizing

Review of Describing a Process

You know that the words below show time order (Chapter 5):

First, . . .
Next, . . .
Then . . .
Finally/Lastly, . . .

The words **after that** also show time order. We use these words in the same way as **next** and **then.**

After that,
Next, } there was music and dancing.
Then

We use **after that, next,** and **then** at the beginning of a sentence. We cannot use them to make two sentences into a single sentence.

Using *before* and *after* To Show Time Order

When we describe a process, we often use dependent clauses beginning with **before** or **after.** These words show time order.

A *clause* is a group of words with a subject and a verb. There are two kinds of clauses: main clauses and dependent clauses. A *main clause* is a separate sentence. A *dependent clause* depends on the main clause; it cannot stand alone.

Exercise 1

Read each of the following clauses. If the clause is a separate sentence and can stand alone, write "main clause" under it. If the clause cannot stand alone, write "dependent clause" under it.

1. The young girl enters the church

    Example: main clause

2. before they eat

    _____

3. after they finish the ceremony

    _____

4. she invites her closest relatives

    _____

5. before the church ceremony begins

    _____

6. her parents embrace her

_____

7. the quincenera wears a beautiful pink dress

_____

8. before they go to the party

_____

Writing a Dependent Clause with *before* or *after*

Look at the sentences below. Each statement has a main clause and a dependent clause.

<u>After the religious ceremony is over</u>, they go to a hall.
(Dependent clause)

<u>Before they go to the party</u>, they pose for photographs.
(Dependent clause)

When the dependent clause comes first, separate it from the main clause with a comma.

Exercise 2

Punctuate the following sentences with a comma where necessary.

1. Before they go to the party they pose for photographs.

2. After they have dinner there is dancing.

3. Before they have the special party they have a church ceremony.

4. After the church ceremony is over her parents embrace her.

5. Before they have a reception they must rent a hall and a band to play music.

6. After the girl and her family arrive at the hall the party can begin.

Use the word in parentheses to combine each pair of sentences into a single sentence. Begin with the dependent clause.

1. You have a religious ceremony.
   You have a dinner and dance. (after)

   Example: _After you have a religious ceremony, you have a dinner and dance._

2. They pose for photographs.
   They go to the party. (before)

   _____

   _____

   _____

3. The guests have dinner. (after)
   The girl starts to dance with her father.

   _____

   _____

   _____

4. The girl dances with her father. (after)
   The other guests dance.

   _____

   _____

   _____

Find the mistakes. There are 10 mistakes in grammar and punctuation. Find and correct them.

First you need to invite your closest relatives, like parents grandparents aunts uncles godparents brothers sisters and close friends. Then, you must decide what food you will give your guests at the dinner. Next, you must pick out a church and a hall. Finally you must pick out a dress. For many girls, this is the importantest thing.

Writing Practice

Choose one of the topics below:
1. A special birthday or other celebration in my country
2. A religious ceremony in my country
3. A wedding reception in my country

1. Pre-writing.

Work with a partner. Tell your partner about a wedding in your country. Then write down what they do first, what comes next, what comes after that, ...

2. Develop an outline.

Number your sentences in the correct order. Then rewrite all the sentences in a paragraph. Use words showing time order. The paragraph outline on the next page will help you.

Paragraph Outline

(Topic sentence) _____.

First, _____.

Next, _____.

After that,/Then _____.

After/Before _____.

Finally, _____.

3. Write a rough draft.

4. Revise your rough draft.

Using the checklist below, check your rough draft or let your partner check it.

Paragraph Checklist

____ Did you give your paragraph a title?
____ Did you indent the first line?
____ Did you write on every other line?
____ Does your paragraph have a topic sentence?
____ Are your ideas in the correct order?
____ Does your paragraph have a concluding sentence?

5. Edit your paragraph.

Work with a partner or your teacher to edit your paragraph. Check spelling, punctuation, vocabulary, and grammar.

6. Write your final copy.

Do you know about these American customs and traditions?

Circle T if the answer is true. Circle F if the answer is false.

1. At the end of a letter or note, an "X" sign means a kiss.   T   F
2. In the United States, you cannot hear the national anthem or song at sports games.   T   F
3. A potluck party is a party where you can play a game and win some money.   T   F
4. It is the custom in the United States to use a toothpick after a meal in front of other people.   T   F
5. In the United States, a bride in her wedding dress must have something old, something new, something borrowed, and something blue.   T   F
6. Leap year is the one year in four when the month of February has twenty-nine days. It is the custom that a woman can ask a man to marry her on February 29.   T   F
7. In the United States, it is the custom to eat with one hand and keep the hand that you do not use on your lap.   T   F
8. In the United States, it is the custom to snap your fingers to get attention.   T   F

Video Activity • Marriages in India

1. In many countries, couples do not marry for love; marriages are arranged by the families of the man and woman. The video describes arranged marriages in India. What are the advantages of these kinds of marriages? Discuss these terms used in the video: *dowry, caste, sentiment, gamble.*

2. As you view the video, listen for the information necessary to answer the following questions.

   a. How many times did the couple in the video meet before agreeing to marry?

   b. What is the percentage of arranged marriages in India?

   c. How are today's arranged marriages different from those of a century ago?

   d. What two customs would India like to get rid of?

   e. What are two reasons parents want arranged marriages?

   f. Is the divorce rate in India higher or lower than the rate in many western countries?

3. After you watch the video, answer the questions above, and discuss the following:

   a. What does this statement from the video mean? "Life's a gamble in any case."

   b. What is your opinion? Are marriages stronger when couples learn to love each other (a) before they get married or (b) after they get married?

Internet Activity

Find a web site with information about a famous custom or tradition in your country or a country you know well. What new facts did you learn? Imagine you are telling someone how to follow this custom. Write down the steps they would have to follow.

Famous People

CHAPTER SEVEN

Louis Braille

Pre-Reading Activity

Discuss these questions.

1. What are the hands in the picture doing?
2. How can blind people read?
3. What do you know about blind people?

Key Vocabulary

Do you know these words? Match the words with the meanings.

1. ____ infection
2. ____ sharp
3. ____ blind
4. ____ tool
5. ____ copy
6. ____ look forward to
7. ____ dots
8. ____ unlucky

a. something you use for doing work
b. not able to see
c. wait with happiness for
d. able to cut easily
e. a disease you get from something or someone
f. having bad things happen by chance
g. make or do something that is the same as something else
h. small round points

Louis Braille

Louis Braille was born near Paris, France, in 1809. When he was a little boy, Louis loved to play with his father's **tools.** One day, when he was four, he was playing with his father's tools when a **sharp** tool went into his left eye. An **infection** started in his left eye and went to the other eye. He was **unlucky.** A few weeks later, Louis was **blind.**

When Louis was ten, his parents took him to a school for blind children in Paris. Louis lived at the school. He was a good student and **looked forward to** the day when he could read. The school had some books that blind people could read. These books had letters that stood out. He had to feel each letter with his fingers. There was one sentence on each page. Just one part of a book weighed 20 pounds. A whole book weighed 400 pounds! By age eleven, Louis had read all fourteen books in the school. He wanted to read more, but there were no more books. So every evening, he tried to find a way for blind people to be able to read books. One day, Captain Charles Barbier, a French soldier, came to speak at the school. Barbier had invented night-writing. This system used **dots** for the letters of the alphabet. Soldiers could feel the dots with their fingers and read with no light. Barbier thought night-writing could also help blind people.

Barbier's system was difficult, but it gave Louis an idea. He worked night after night to make a simple system with dots. By age fifteen, he had finished his system. He showed it to other students in the school, and they loved it. They called it Braille, after him. At age seventeen, Louis graduated from the school and became a teacher there. In his free time, he **copied** books into Braille. Someone read to Louis while he made the dots. He copied the books of Shakespeare and other writers into Braille. The students read all the books and wanted more. The school did not want a fifteen-year-old boy's invention to be better than their own heavy books and would not let students read Braille books. Nevertheless, the students continued to read them. Finally, after twenty years, the school agreed to use Braille.

Louis Braille spent the rest of his life trying to tell the world about Braille. But nobody cared. Louis was unlucky again. He became very sick. Even when he was sick in his bed, he continued to write books in Braille for the students at his school. A few years later, Louis Braille died at age forty-three. Two years after he died, schools for the blind began to use his system.

Today, we use Braille not only to write words in all languages, but also to write math and music. Blind people send Braille greeting cards, wear Braille watches, type on Braille keyboards, and take elevators with Braille controls. Louis Braille had no idea how many people he had helped. On the door of the house where he was born are the words "He opened the doors of knowledge to all those who cannot see."

Vocabulary

Meaning

Complete the sentences with the following words.

an infection	copied
dots	blind
sharp	unlucky
tools	looked forward to

1. When Louis was a child, he played with his father's _____.

2. A _____ tool went into his eye.

3. Louis got _____ in his eye.

4. Louis became _____ when he was four years old.

5. Louis liked school and _____ the day when he could read.

6. Barbier's system used _____.

7. Louis was _____ again in life.

8. Louis _____ other books into Braille.

Vocabulary Activity

Answer the questions. Use complete sentences.

1. What is the name of something sharp you use?

_____

_____

2. What day or number is unlucky for you?

_____

_____

3. What do you copy when you are in class?

_____

_____

4. What food or drink do you look forward to having when you get home?

_____

_____

5. What color stick does a blind person use?

_____

_____

6. Where do you put a dot when you write?

_____

_____

7. What do you take when you have an infection?

_____

_____

8. What tool does a painter use?

_____

_____

Comprehension

Looking for the Main Ideas

Circle the letter of the best answer.

1. When Louis was four, he ——————.
   - a. became blind
   - b. had sharp tools
   - c. went to school
   - d. read books

2. Charles Barbier ——————.
   - a. had an infection
   - b. invented night-writing
   - c. visited soldiers
   - d. became a teacher

3. By age fifteen, Louis ——————.
   - a. had died
   - b. was difficult
   - c. made a new system of reading
   - d. had copied many books

Looking for Details

One word in each sentence is not correct. Rewrite the sentence with the correct word.

1. When Louis was four, a blind tool went into his eye.

   _____

   _____

2. Louis went to a school for unlucky children in Paris.

   _____

   _____

3. Barbier's system used tools for the letters of the alphabet.

   _____

   _____

4. Barbier thought his system could help blind people to play.

   _____

   _____

5. Louis died at age thirty-four.

    _____

    _____

6. Today, we use Braille not only to write words in all languages, but also to write art and music.

    _____

    _____

Discussion

Discuss these questions with your classmates.

1. Do you know of other famous blind people? How are blind people special?

2. Louis Braille was unlucky. Do you know another unlucky person? Explain.

Now read the following paragraph written by a student.

Model Paragraph

My Sister Liz

My sister Liz was born lucky. She has a beautiful smile. When she does something bad, she smiles and my parents are not angry. She eats a lot and does not get fat. Her favorite meal is a double cheeseburger with French fries, a milkshake, and an ice cream sundae. She does not study hard but always gets good grades. After school, she does her homework in five minutes while she watches television at the same time. In conclusion, I believe that some people are born lucky, and some are not.

Organizing

Unity

As you know, a good paragraph has three parts: a topic sentence, supporting sentences, and a concluding sentence. But a good paragraph also has unity.

Unity means that all of the supporting sentences are about the controlling idea in the topic sentence. Think about the model paragraph above.

Topic sentence: My sister Liz was <u>born lucky</u>.
            (Controlling idea)

Main supporting sentences:

1.   She has a beautiful smile.
2.   She eats a lot and does not get fat.
3.   She does not study hard but always gets good grades.

This paragraph has unity. All the supporting sentences are about why she was born lucky.

Irrelevant Sentences

When a sentence does not belong in a paragraph, we say that it is an *irrelevant sentence.*

Example:

My sister Jamie is very shy. When there are other people around, she speaks very little. Sometimes she does not speak at all and even runs away. She is very quiet at home and at school. You do not even know she is there sometimes. She is shy about her body, too. She never goes to the beach or swimming pool. But she like ice cream and cookies.

Irrelevant sentence: But she likes ice cream and cookies.

The sentence "But she likes ice cream and cookies" does not belong in the paragraph. It does not talk about why she is shy.

Exercise 1

Underline the irrelevant sentences in the following short paragraphs.

1. George has not been lucky in school this year. He got sick and missed classes and could not take his finals. He also lost his books. These were not only his textbooks but also his notebooks. Everybody likes George because he will go out of his way to help people.

2. My roommate Tony is very untidy. He has brown hair and blue eyes. He leaves his laundry on the floor. When he cooks, he never washes the dishes. For a while, he had a bicycle on his bed. It is not surprising that Tony can never find anything.

3. My Uncle Conrad is very clumsy. When he drinks coffee, he always spills some on his shirt. In the shopping mall, he walks into other people all the time. He has size 14 feet. Last time he came to our house, he sat on the cat.

4. Aunt Dotty loves adventure. On her sixtieth birthday, she went mountain climbing in the Alps. On her seventieth birthday, she went on a trip to the North Pole. When she was eighty, she drove alone across the United States. She loves to eat chocolate. We all wonder what she will do when she is ninety.

Exercise 2

Find the mistakes. There are 10 mistakes in grammar, punctuation, and capitalization. Find and correct them.

The braille family lived in a village near paris france. There were four childrens, and Louis was the most youngest. The boy was very smart and his father hope he would grow up to be a teacher. But then a terrible accident happened and Louis became Blind.

Writing Practice

Choose one of the topics below:
1. A person who is lucky or unlucky
2. A good or bad quality of a friend or family member
3. A pet cat or dog

1. Pre-writing.

Work with a partner or alone.

a. Write down a topic sentence about a person or animal. You can follow this outline for a topic sentence:

What person /animal is to you	+	name	+	verb	+	adjective
My pet dog		Rex		is		very lazy.

b. List as many points as you can about the person or animal.

c. Go over each point on your list. Ask yourself, "Does this support the controlling idea?" Cross out the points that do not.

2. Develop an outline.

a. Organize your ideas. List the points in the order in which you will write about them in your paragraph.

b. Make a more detailed outline. The paragraph outline on the next page will help you.

Paragraph Outline

(Topic sentence) _____.

(Supporting sentence 1) _____.

(Supporting detail[s]) _____.

(Supporting sentence 2) _____.

(Supporting detail[s]) _____.

(Supporting sentence 3) _____.

(Supporting detail[s]) _____.

(Concluding sentence) _____.

3. Write a rough draft.

4. Revise your rough draft.

> Using the checklist below, check your rough draft or let your partner check it.

> **Paragraph Checklist**
> _____ Did you give your paragraph a title?
> _____ Did you indent the first line?
> _____ Did you write on every other line?
> _____ Does your paragraph have a topic sentence?
> _____ Does your topic sentence have a controlling idea?
> _____ Do your other sentences support your topic sentence?
> _____ Are your ideas in the correct order?
> _____ Does your paragraph have a concluding sentence?

5. Edit your paragraph.

> Work with a partner or your teacher to edit your paragraph. Correct spelling, punctuation, vocabulary, and grammar.

6. Write your final copy.

CHAPTER EIGHT

The World's Most Unusual Millionaire

Hetty Green, an unusual millionaire

Pre-Reading Activity

Discuss these questions.

1. Who are some famous millionaires today?
2. What kinds of things do they own?
3. Imagine you are a millionaire. What will you spend your money on? Check the boxes, and discuss your answers.
   - ☐ expensive car
   - ☐ beautiful home
   - ☐ other
   - ☐ expensive clothes
   - ☐ nice vacations
4. Would you give money to charity (organizations to help the sick and poor)? Why or why not?
5. The woman in the picture was a millionaire. What do you expect a millionaire to look like?

Key Vocabulary

Do you know these words? Match the words with the meanings.

1. ____ stingy
2. ____ waste
3. ____ refuse
4. ____ raw
5. ____ refund
6. ____ laundry
7. ____ space
8. ____ medical treatment

a. say that you will not do or take something
b. care given by doctors
c. not wanting to spend or give away money
d. empty area
e. not use; use when it is not necessary
f. not cooked
g. place where they wash and iron clothes
h. money you get back for something you bought

The World's Most Unusual Millionaire

Hetty Robinson was born in 1834. When her parents died, she was thirty years old. They left her $10 million ($185 million in today's dollars). She was very good at business and soon made more money. Hetty was famous as the richest woman in the United States, but she was also famous because she was very **stingy.**

Even when she was young, she was stingy. For instance, on her twenty-first birthday, she **refused** to light the candles on her birthday cake because she did not want to **waste** them. The next day, she cleaned the candles and returned them to the store to get a **refund.**

Hetty always thought men wanted to marry her for her money. Finally, at the age of thirty-three, she decided to get married because she did not want her relatives to get her money. She married Edward Green, who was a millionaire. They had a son and a daughter. Soon after, Hetty divorced him because she did not agree with him about money matters.

Hetty was even stingy with her own child. For example, when her son hurt his knee in an accident, Hetty did not call a doctor. She tried to take care of it herself. When her son's knee didn't get better, she dressed him in old clothes and took him to a free clinic. The doctors recognized her and asked for money. Hetty refused to pay and took her son home. The boy did not get **medical treatment**, and a few years later his leg was amputated.

Hetty was stingy with herself, too. For example, she always wore the same black dress. As the years passed by, the color of the dress changed from black to green and then brown. When the dress became dirty, she went to a cheap **laundry** and told them to wash only the bottom where it was dirty, and she waited until it was ready. Her undergarments were old newspapers she got from the streets. She rented a cheap apartment with no heat in New Jersey because she did not want to pay taxes in New York. Then she traveled on the train to her office in New York. Her office was a **space** in a bank, which the bank gave to her for free. All she ate was **raw** onions and cold oatmeal. She was too stingy to spend money to heat her food. Sometimes, to heat her oatmeal, she put it on the office heater because that was free. She also ate cookies, but regular cookies were too expensive for her, so she walked a long way to get broken cookies, which were much cheaper. One time, she spent half the night looking for a two-cent stamp.

When Hetty Green died in 1916, she had no friends. She left more than $100 million (over $17 billion today) to her son and daughter. Her son and daughter were not stingy like Hetty, and they spent the money freely.

Vocabulary

Meaning

Complete the sentences with the following words.

waste	medical treatment
laundry	space
refund	stingy
raw	refused

1. Hetty did not like to spend money; she was ——————.

2. Hetty went to the —————— to have the bottom part of her dress washed.

3. On her twenty-first birthday, Hetty —————— to light the candles on her cake.

4. Hetty liked to use everything. She did not like to —————— anything.

5. She went back to the store to get a —————— of the money she paid for the birthday candles.

6. Her son hurt his knee, but he did not get ——————.

7. The bank gave Hetty a —————— to use as her office.

8. Hetty did not cook onions; she ate them ——————.

Vocabulary Activity

Work with a partner. Read the questions and add the letters to complete the answers.

1. What does a **stingy** person *not* like to spend?

   M — — — Y

2. What is the name for a green **space** in a big city?

   P — R —

3. What **medical treatment** does a doctor usually give when you are sick?

   M — D — — — T — — N

4. What is something many business people do not like to **waste**?

   — — M —

5. What is a vegetable most people do *not* eat **raw**?

   P — — A T —

Now make a sentence with each of the words in bold.

Example: <u>A stingy person does not like to spend money.</u>

Comprehension

Looking for the Main Ideas

Circle the letter of the best answer.

1. Hetty was a very rich woman, but she was —————.
   a. stingy
   b. short
   c. green
   d. old

2. Hetty married _____.
   a. for love
   b. to have children
   c. so that her relatives would not get her money
   d. so that she would not be lonely

3. Hetty was even stingy with _____.
   a. Edward Green
   b. her own child
   c. her leg
   d. her parents

Looking for Details

Circle T if the answer is true. Circle F if the answer is false.

1.	Hetty's parents died when she was thirty.	T	F
2.	Hetty ate mostly raw onions and cold oatmeal.	T	F
3.	Hetty called the doctor for her son.	T	F
4.	Hetty lived in New York.	T	F
5.	Hetty lived in an apartment with no heat.	T	F
6.	When Hetty died, she left $10 million.	T	F

Discussion

Discuss these questions with your classmates.

1. What famous person do you know of who had a bad characteristic? Say what he or she did.
2. Describe some other types of people who are not very nice, and say why.
3. Some people are stingy about some things but spend money on other things. Are you this way? Give examples.

Describe a stingy person you know.

1. Identify the person.

    Example: <u>Mr. Norton lives in my apartment building.</u>

    _____

    _____

2. What does this person NOT like to spend money on (for example, food, new clothes, restaurants, gifts)?

    Example: <u>This person does not like to spend money on electricity.</u>

    _____

    _____

3. Give an example.

    Example: <u>When I go to see him in his apartment in the evening, it is always dark. The curtains are open so that he gets light from the street.</u>

    _____

    _____

Compare with your classmates. Who has the best example of a stingy person?

Now read the following paragraph written by a student.

Model Paragraph

My Selfish Brother

My brother is very selfish. He does not want to share things with other people. For example, when he buys a chocolate bar, he puts it in a secret place. Then he eats it all, by himself. He never helps anyone. He says he is busy. For example, a game of Nintendo makes him very busy. He does not care if something he does bothers other people. For instance, last night he played loud rock 'n' roll music until four o'clock in the morning. In conclusion, I think my brother is selfish and will always be selfish.

Organizing

Giving Examples

To introduce an example in your paragraph, you can use the following:

For example, . . .

or

For instance, . . .

1. Underline the words showing examples in the reading.
2. Underline the words showing examples in the model paragraph.
3. Look at the use of the comma with the words showing examples.
4. Now go back and circle all the commas with the words showing examples in the reading and in the model paragraph.

In the model paragraph, the writer used **for example** or **for instance** to give details about supporting sentences.

Topic sentence: My brother is very selfish.

Supporting sentence: He does not want to share things with other people.

Detail or example of supporting sentence: For example, when he buys a chocolate bar, he puts it in a secret place.

For example and **for instance** have the same meaning. When your sentence begins with **for example** or **for instance**, put a comma after these words.

> **For example,** when he buys a chocolate bar, he puts it in a secret place.

or

> **For instance,** when he buys a chocolate bar, he puts it in a secret place.

A sentence that begins with **for example** or **for instance** must be a complete sentence.

> For example, Hetty Green. (Not correct)
> For example, Hetty Green was a millionaire. (Correct)

Exercise 2

The following sentences are not complete or have mistakes. Write out the correct sentences.

1. For example he gets food all over his shirt.

   _____

2. For instance, washes dishes.

   _____

3. For example: she never writes down my telephone messages.

   _____

4. For instance, a doctor.

   _____

5. For instance—she always leaves the bathroom in a mess.

   _____

A name of a person or a thing can follow the words **for example** and **for instance.**

Women became leaders in the last century. **For example,** Margaret Thatcher and Golda Meir were both prime ministers of their countries.

Work alone, with a partner, or in a group. Think of examples for the following statements. Add more if you can.

1. There are many famous millionaires today. For example, _____ and _____ are millionaires.

2. There were some famous people who were very stingy. For instance, _____ and _____ were stingy.

3. Some people in history did very bad things. For example, _____ and _____ did terrible things.

Write a complete sentence as an example for each statement. Use **for instance** or **for example** in the correct form.

1. My grandfather is very forgetful.

    _____

    _____

2. My English teacher has an excellent memory.

    _____

    _____

3. My sister is not an electrician, but she can fix many electrical things in the house.

    _____

    _____

Find the mistakes. There are 10 mistakes in grammar, punctuation, capitalization, and spelling. Find and correct them.

Howard hughes was born in texas in 1906. He was one of the richest men in the world but he was very strange. For example he eats the same dinner every night: a steak a potato and 12 peas. Later in his life, he became even stranger. For instance: he did not wear clothes and did not cut his hare. Hughes dies without any friends in 1976.

Writing Practice

Choose one of the topics below:

1. A stingy person I know
2. A person who has a bad characteristic (for example, selfish, inconsiderate, lazy, etc.)
3. An unusual person

1. Pre-writing.

Work with a partner or alone.

a. Write down a topic sentence about a person. (Choose from the topics above.)
b. List as many points as you can about the person.
c. Go over each point on your list. Ask yourself, "Does this support the controlling idea?" Cross out the points that do not.
d. Think of an example for each point. If you cannot find an example, cross out the point.

2. Develop an outline.

a. Organize your ideas. List the points in the order you will write about them. You should have two or three points.
b. Make a more detailed outline. The paragraph outline on the next page will help you.

Paragraph Outline

(Topic sentence) _____.

(Supporting sentence 1) For example, _____.

_____.

(Supporting sentence 2) For instance, _____.

_____.

(Supporting sentence 3) For example, _____.

_____.

(Concluding sentence) _____.

3. Write a rough draft.

4. Revise your rough draft.

> Using the checklist below, check your rough draft or let your partner check it.

> **Paragraph Checklist**
> _____ Did you give your paragraph a title?
> _____ Did you indent the first line?
> _____ Did you write on every other line?
> _____ Does your paragraph have a topic sentence?
> _____ Does your topic sentence have a controlling idea?
> _____ Do your other sentences support your topic sentence?
> _____ Are your ideas in the correct order?
> _____ Do you have examples?
> _____ Does your paragraph have a concluding sentence?

5. Edit your paragraph.

> Work with a partner or your teacher to edit your paragraph. Correct spelling, punctuation, vocabulary, and grammar.

6. Write your final copy.

Who are they?

1.

This president never smiled in any of his pictures. Who was he?

2.

This composer died a poor man at age thirty-five. Who was he?

3.

This African-American leader was killed in 1968. Who was he?

4.

This blind and deaf woman went to college and wrote books. Who was she?

5.

This nun went to India to look after the poor, the sick, and the dying. Who was she?

6.

This woman wrote the story of Frankenstein. Who was she?

Video Activity • Famous Movie Stars

1. Some movie stars from the United States are famous all over the world. Who are a few of the most famous ones? Who are the most famous African-American actors? What movies have they been in?

2. The video shows several famous actors/actresses who were nominated for Academy Awards in 2002. Can you match the stars with the movies below? Put the correct letter on the line in front of the movie title. The first one is done.

   _c_ 1. *Ali*   a. Denzel Washington
   ___ 2. *A Beautiful Mind* b. Nicole Kidman
   ___ 3. *Moulin Rouge*   c. Will Smith
   ___ 4. *Monster's Ball*   d. Sissy Spacek
   ___ 5. *In the Bedroom*   e. Russell Crowe
   ___ 6. *Training Days*   f. Halle Berry

3. Check your answers after you watch the video. What actor was left out of the nominations even though he played important roles in three movies during the year? Watch the video again if necessary to find out.

Internet Activity

Go to the Internet to find out more about a famous person whom you admire. Write a paragraph describing his or her personality, and give examples to support your description.

Nature's Disasters

CHAPTER NINE

Lightning

Pre-Reading Activity

Discuss these questions.

1. What is happening in the picture?
2. How can lightning be dangerous?
3. What can you do to protect against a lightning strike?

Key Vocabulary

Do you know these words? Match the words with the meanings.

1. ____ lightning bolt
2. ____ amaze
3. ____ injured
4. ____ explode
5. ____ protect
6. ____ attract
7. ____ shelter
8. ____ frighten

a. make someone or something want to come there
b. bright flash of light you see in the sky during a storm
c. stop someone or something from being harmed
d. hurt
e. blow apart, like a bomb
f. building or place where you are safe from harm
g. surprise greatly
h. make afraid

Lightning

Every second of every day, all over the world, there are more than 100 **lightning bolts.** That's about ten million lightning bolts in one day! Lightning **amazes** us, but it can also **frighten** us. We have good reason to be afraid of lightning. Every year, about 100 people in the United States and Canada die from lightning, and another 300 are **injured.** It is strange that of all the people who die from lightning, 84 percent are men. Lightning is the main cause of forest fires; it starts more than 9,000 fires each year.

Lightning is electricity inside a cloud. Scientists do not know exactly what makes this electricity. But they know that the electricity inside a cloud can be as much as 100 million volts. From this extremely strong electricity, a lightning bolt, like a streak of bright light, comes down from the sky. Its temperature can reach 50,000 degrees Fahrenheit within a few millionths of a second. That's almost five times the temperature on the sun's surface. The lightning bolt is very quick. It can move at a speed of 87,000 miles per second. A rocket traveling at this speed would reach the moon in 2.5 seconds. With the lightning bolt, we usually hear thunder, which is the sound of hot air **exploding.** Lightning and thunder happen at exactly the same time, but we see lightning first because light travels a million times faster than sound.

Lightning often strikes tall buildings. However, many buildings have lightning rods to **protect** them from lightning. When lightning strikes, the electricity goes safely down the metal rod to the ground. Benjamin Franklin, the American statesman, invented the lightning rod in 1760. That is why buildings like the Empire State Building in New York City are safe. Lightning may hit this building as many as twelve times in twenty minutes and as often as 500 times a year. Airplanes are not as easy to protect as buildings, and accidents do happen. In 1963, a Boeing 707 jet was hit by lightning and crashed. Eighty-one people died.

If you see thunder and lightning coming, here are some things you can do to protect yourself. Go inside a house, get into a car, or go under a bridge. If you cannot find **shelter,** go to the lowest point on the ground. If you are outside, remember that trees **attract** lightning, especially tall trees. Never go under a tall tree that stands alone. If you are in a field, drop to your knees, bend forward, and put your hands on your knees. Do not lie down because the wet ground can carry lightning. Stay away from a lake, an ocean, or any other water. Don't touch or go near anything metal, such as a metal fence, golf clubs, and bicycles, because metal attracts lightning very quickly. Don't use a telephone except in an emergency.

They say that lightning never hits the same place twice, but this is not true. One man, Roy Sullivan, was hit by lightning seven different times in his life. He was injured each time but did not die. He died in 1983, but not from lightning. He killed himself because he loved a woman, but she didn't love him!

Vocabulary

Meaning

Complete the sentences with the following words.

frightened	injured
protects	shelter
attract	lightning bolts
amaze	exploding

1. There are millions of _____ every day.

2. A sky with lightning can _____ you.

3. Many people are _____ when they see lightning because it is dangerous.

4. When lightning strikes people, they can be _____ or die.

5. Thunder sounds as if fireworks are _____.

6. A lightning rod _____ buildings from lightning strikes.

7. In a storm, you should find _____ from the bad weather.

8. Tall buildings _____ lightning strikes.

Vocabulary Activity

Answer the questions. Use complete sentences.

1. What is something you can wear or carry that protects you from the rain?

    _____

    _____

2. What kind of weather situation frightens you?

    _____

    _____

3. What modern invention amazes you?

    _____

    _____

4. You are in the country, and it starts to rain. Where can you go for shelter?

    _____

    _____

5. What is something that can explode?

    _____

    _____

6. In what situation can a person be injured?

    _____

    _____

7. What kind of place attracts you for a vacation?

    _____

    _____

Comprehension

Looking for the Main Ideas

Circle the letter of the best answer.

1. Lightning _____.
    a. is not dangerous
    b. kills only men
    c. kills and injures many people
    d. happens about 100 times a day

2. Lightning _____.
    a. and thunder happen at the same time
    b. is as hot as the surface of the sun
    c. comes after thunder
    d. is hot air exploding

3. Lightning often strikes _____.
    a. Americans
    b. tall men
    c. tall buildings
    d. New York City

Looking for Details

Use complete sentences to answer the questions.

1. How many people die from lightning in the United States and Canada every year?

    _____

    _____

2. Why do we see lightning before we hear thunder?

    _____

    _____

3. Why is it not a good idea to touch metal when there's lightning?

_____

_____

4. Which building in New York City gets hit by lightning 500 times a year?

_____

_____

5. Who invented the lightning rod?

_____

_____

6. How did Roy Sullivan die?

_____

_____

Discussion

Discuss these questions with your classmates.

1. Why do you think more men than women die from lightning?
2. Almost every day, there is a natural disaster in the news. It could be a hurricane, a snowstorm, a flood, or an earthquake. What makes you most afraid?
3. The disasters that we are most likely to remember are those that happen closest to where we live. Can you remember a disaster (fire, plane crash, etc.) that happened near where you lived? Tell about it.

Now read the following paragraph written by a student.

Model Paragraph

A Terrifying Day

October 1, 1987, was a terrifying day for me. It was 7:30 on a Thursday morning in Mexico. I was alone because my parents were out of town. Suddenly, the room started to shake. Some dishes fell to the floor. I did not know what to do, so I got under a table. A few minutes later, I came out and tried to turn on the television, but the electricity was off. After that, I tried the telephone, but it did not work. Shortly after, the neighbors came to see if I was all right. Finally, at about 9:00 A.M., the telephone rang. It was my mother from Mexico City. She was more frightened than I was.

Organizing

A Narrative Paragraph

The paragraph you just read is a *narrative paragraph.* A narrative paragraph tells a story about something that happened. In a narrative paragraph, you must use a good time order for your sentences. This means that the sentences must be in the order in which the story happened.

The following sentences are about a terrifying day, but they are not in the correct time order. Number them in the correct order.

a.   I got under the table.

b.   I came out and tried the telephone, but it did not work.

c.   Shortly after that, the neighbors came to see if I was all right.

d.   The room started to shake.

The next step is to add words that show time order to connect your sentences. These words show the order in which things happened in time.

Words Showing Time Order

October 1, 1987, . . .
At 5 P.M., . . .
Suddenly, . . .
A few minutes later, . . .
After that, . . .
Shortly after that, . . .
Finally, . . .

Now underline the words showing time order in the model paragraph.

Punctuation

The Comma (,) with Time and Place Expressions

Look at the words showing time order. Look at the use of the comma after words showing time order. Now go back to the model paragraph and circle all the commas after the words showing time order.

We also use a comma with dates and place names.

Dates

1.   We use a comma to separate a date from a year:

I came to the United States on March 4, 1990.
They were married on July 26, 1987.

2. We use a comma after the year when a sentence continues:
   October 1, 1987, was the day of the earthquake.
   On March 27, 1964, a big earthquake hit Alaska.

Place Names

1. We use a comma to separate a city from a state or a city from a country:

   We were at home in Anchorage, Alaska.
   I come from Tokyo, Japan.

2. We use a comma after a state or country when the sentence continues:

   Crescent City, California, is on the coast.

Exercise 2

Put a comma where necessary in the following sentences.

1. The San Francisco earthquake hit on the morning of April 18 1906.

2. On November 4 1951 a tidal wave hit Hawaii.

3. A tidal wave hit Crescent City California.

4. The biggest earthquake recorded in North America was the earthquake of March 27 1964.

5. Suddenly people heard a noise like thunder.

6. An earthquake hit Armenia on December 7 1988.

7. In Yokohama Japan there were a lot of fires.

8. Valdez Alaska was ten feet higher after the earthquake.

9. A few minutes later buildings fell.

10. Shortly after a tidal wave hit Alaska.

Find the mistakes. There are 10 mistakes in punctuation and capitalization. Find and correct them.

In the United States, the States with the greatest number of deaths from lightning are Florida texas and north Carolina. Avoid these states, especially in June, which is the worst month for lightning. The other bad months are august, july april and September.

Writing Practice

Choose one of the topics below:
1. A frightening day
2. A dangerous experience
3. A strange experience

1. Pre-writing.

Work with a partner. Tell your partner about your experience. Then write answers to the questions below.

a. When and where did the experience occur?

_____

_____

b. What happened?

_____

_____

c. What happened after that?

_____

_____

2. Develop an outline.

Write the sentences in the order in which they happened. Then use the words showing time order. The paragraph outline on the next page will help you.

Paragraph Outline

      (Date) was a   day for me. I was

because   .

Suddenly,   .

A few minutes later,   .

Shortly after that,   .

Finally,   .

3. Write a rough draft.

4. Revise your rough draft.

   Using the checklist below, check your rough draft or let your partner check it.

   Paragraph Checklist
   ____ Did you give your paragraph a title?
   ____ Did you indent the first line?
   ____ Did you write on every other line? (Look at pages 8–9 for instructions on paragraph form.)
   ____ Does your paragraph have a topic sentence?
   ____ Does your topic sentence have a controlling idea?
   ____ Do your other sentences support your topic sentence?
   ____ Are your ideas in the correct order?
   ____ Does your paragraph have a concluding sentence?

5. Edit your paragraph.

   Work with a partner or your teacher to edit your paragraph. Correct spelling, punctuation, vocabulary, and grammar.

6. Write your final copy.

CHAPTER TEN

Killer Bees

Pre-Reading

Discuss these questions.

1. How are bees useful to people?
2. Are you afraid of bees? Why or why not?
3. When do bees sting a person?

Key Vocabulary

Do you know these words? Match the words with the meanings.

1. ____ breed   a. move toward violently
2. ____ attack   b. produce young
3. ____ spread   c. get away
4. ____ escape   d. cover a larger area
5. ____ tell the difference   e. bright, filled with light
6. ____ shiny   f. know one thing from another

Killer Bees

Killer bees started in Brazil in 1957. A scientist in Sao Paulo wanted bees to make more honey, so he put forty-six African bees in with some Brazilian bees. The bees started to **breed** and make a new kind of bee. However, the new bees were a mistake. They did not want to make more honey; they wanted to **attack.** Then, by accident, twenty-six African bees **escaped** and bred with the Brazilian bees outside.

Scientists could not control the problem. The bees **spread.** They went from Brazil to Venezuela and then to Central America. Now they are in North America. They travel about 390 miles a year. Each group of bees, or colony, grows to four times its old size in a year. This means that there will be one million new colonies in five years.

Killer bees are very dangerous, and people are right to be afraid of them. When killer bees attack people, they attack in great numbers and often seriously hurt or kill people. Four hundred bee stings can kill a person. A total of 8,000 bee stings is not unusual for a killer bee attack. In fact, a student in Costa Rica had 10,000 stings and died. Often, the bees attack for no reason. They may attack because of a strong smell that is good or bad or because a person is wearing a dark color, has dark hair, or is wearing some kind of **shiny** jewelry.

What can you do if you see killer bees coming toward you? The first thing you can do is run—as fast as you can. Killer bees do not move very fast, but they will follow you up to one mile. Then you must go into the nearest house or tent. Do not jump into water. The bees will wait for you to come out of the water. Killer bees will try to attack the head or the face, so cover your head with a handkerchief or a coat. You may even take off your shirt and cover your head. Stings to your chest and back are not as dangerous as stings to your head and face. However, if the bees sting you many times, you must get medical attention immediately.

How are killer bees different from normal honey bees? Killer bees are a little smaller than regular bees, but only an expert can **tell the difference.** Killer bees get angry more easily and attack more often than honey bees. Killer bees attack and sting in great numbers. Like honey bees, each killer bee can sting only one time, and the female bee dies after it stings. Killer bees also make honey, but a honey bee makes five times more honey than a killer bee.

Up to now, killer bees have killed about 1,000 people and over 100,000 cows in the Americas. In the United States alone, five people have died from killer bee stings since 1990. The first American died from bee stings in Texas in 1993. From Texas, the bees moved to Nevada, New Mexico, Arizona, and then Southern California. Where will they go next?

Vocabulary

Meaning

Complete the sentences with the following words.

breed	attack
escaped	shiny
spread	tell the difference

1. It is not easy to ——————— between a honey bee and a killer bee because they look almost the same.

2. Killer bees ——————— people and animals for no reason.

3. Twenty-six African bees ——————— outside.

4. The African bees and the Brazilian bees started to ——————— and make a new kind of bee.

5. The new bees went from one country to another. They ——————— quickly.

6. Killer bees attack people who are wearing ——————— objects like jewelry.

Vocabulary Activity

Answer the questions. Use complete sentences.

1. What animal breeds quickly?

_____

2. What dangerous animal may attack people?

_____

3. What disease spreads easily?

_____

4. What kinds of animals are dangerous if they escape?

_____

5. What shiny pieces of jewelry do people wear?

_____

6. How can you tell the difference between a glass cup and a plastic cup?

_____

Comprehension

Looking for the Main Ideas

Circle the letter of the best answer.

1. A scientist wanted bees _____.
   a. to go to Africa
   b. to make more honey
   c. to attack
   d. to breed more

2. Scientists ─────────.
    a. could not control the problem
    b. went to Brazil
    c. grew every year
    d. traveled to North America

3. People are afraid of killer bees because they ─────────.
    a. sting
    b. attack and sting in large groups
    c. attack and die
    d. follow you

Looking for Details

Answer the questions with complete sentences.

1. Where did the killer bees go after they left Central America?

    _____

2. What colors do killer bees like to attack?

    _____

3. What part of the body do killer bees try to attack?

    _____

4. How many times does each killer bee sting?

    _____

5. When did the first American die from killer bees?

    _____

6. How many people have died from killer bees up to now?

    _____

Discussion

Discuss these questions with your classmates.

1. Have you been stung by a bee? What happened?
2. What is a good thing to do when a bee stings you?
3. What insects do you have in your country? Are these insects a problem?
4. What other insects or animals are you afraid of?

Now read the following paragraph written by a student.

Model Paragraph

Cockroaches

Cockroaches have become a major problem in our building for several reasons. First, cockroaches (or roaches) carry germs and disease. Because roaches inhabit areas where there is food, we may get sick from the food we eat. Second, roaches eat everything. They eat not only food but also glue, paint, clothes, wallpaper, and even plastic. There is a feeling of horror and disgust because everything in our home is destroyed by roaches. They even live in and eat the television set. Finally, roaches are indestructible. Nothing can kill the roaches in our building. All the chemical powders and sprays we have tried on them are no good. They always come back. It is either them or us, so we have decided to move out.

Organizing

Giving Reasons

In this lesson, you will learn how to *give reasons* for a situation. Usually, there is more than one reason for a situation. It is important to look at all the reasons. When there are many reasons, there is usually one that is most important.

When you write your reasons, remember the following:

1. Think of or discuss all the reasons. There is probably more than one.

2. Support your reasons. Give examples.

3. State your most important reason last. This will make your paragraph more interesting. If you give your most important reason first, the reader may not feel it necessary to read the rest of your paragraph.

Transitions for Giving Reasons: *because*

Because answers the question "Why?" **Because** comes before the part of the sentence that gives the reason. The reason can come before or after the statement.

Examples:

Statement: We may get sick from the food we eat.

Reason: Roaches inhabit areas where there is food.

We may get sick from the food we eat **because** roaches inhabit areas where there is food.

or

Because roaches inhabit areas where there is food, we may get sick from the food we eat.

Note: Use a comma after the reason if you start the sentence with **because.**

Exercise 1

Join the sentences with **because.** Write each sentence in two ways. First use **because** in the middle. Then use **because** in the beginning.

1. There is a feeling of disgust. Everything in our home is destroyed by roaches.

   _____

   _____

2. We are going to move out. The roaches are not moving out.

   _____

   _____

3. Nothing can kill roaches. Roaches are indestructible.

_____

_____

4. People are afraid of the killer bees. The bees attack more often than a normal bee.

_____

_____

5. The killer bees are spreading. Scientists cannot control them.

_____

_____

Exercise 2

Find the mistakes. There are 10 mistakes in grammar, punctuation, and capitalization. Find and correct them.

A man from texas died after he had been stung forty times as he was trying to remove a nest. Since January 1 2000, there has been two serious attacks in las Vegas. Bees stung a 79-year-old man thirty times, but he lived. In march bees covered a 77-year-old-woman who is walking down the street. The bees were attracted to something she was carrying in her bag. Firefighters covered the woman with water to remove more than 200 bees from her. Bees stung the woman more than 500 times, but she lived two.

Writing Practice

Choose one of the topics below:

1. An animal or insect I dislike
2. An animal or insect that is a problem
3. A disease that is a problem

1. Pre-writing.

Work with a group, a partner, or alone.

a. Write your topic at the top of your paper.

b. Then think of as many reasons about the topic as you can. Write every word or phrase that comes into your mind about the topic. Write down as much information as you can.

c. Write your ideas in any order you like. Do not worry about whether or not the idea is important. Write it down.

2. Develop an outline.

a. Organize your ideas.

Step 1: Write the main idea sentence.

Step 2: Pick the best reasons from the ones you wrote.

Step 3: Order your reasons. Don't forget to put your most important reason last.

Step 4: Remember to use these transitions for giving reasons:

The first reason is . . .	or	First, . . .
The second reason is . . .	or	Second, . . .
The final reason is . . .	or	Finally, . . .

b. Make a more detailed outline. The paragraph outline on the next page will help you.

Paragraph Outline

	_____ for several reasons.
(Supporting fact)	The first reason is _____ .
(Supporting fact)	The second reason is _____ .
(Supporting fact)	The final reason is _____ .
(Concluding sentence)	_____ .

3. Write a rough draft.

4. Revise your rough draft.

> Using the checklist below, check your rough draft or let your partner check it.

> ### Paragraph Checklist
> _____ Did you give your paragraph a title?
> _____ Did you indent the first line?
> _____ Did you write on every other line? (Look at pages 8–9 for instructions on paragraph form.)
> _____ Does your paragraph have a topic sentence?
> _____ Does your topic sentence have a controlling idea?
> _____ Do your other sentences support your topic sentence?
> _____ Are your ideas in the correct order?
> _____ Does your paragraph have a concluding sentence?

5. Edit your paragraph.

> Work with a partner or your teacher to edit your paragraph. Check spelling, punctuation, vocabulary, and grammar.

6. Write your final copy.

What do you know about insects?

Circle the correct answer.

1. How many different species of insects are living on earth?
   a. One million
   b. Three million

2. How many times its body length can a flea jump?
   a. Twenty times
   b. Sixty times

3. Most animals have changed over the last million years. But cockroaches have not changed in any way for a long time. How long?
   a. 250 million years
   b. 50 million years

4. Some worms have more than one heart. How many hearts can some worms have?
   a. Five
   b. Ten

5. How many stomachs does a honey bee have?
   a. One
   b. Two

6. How many times its body weight can an ant lift?
   a. Fifty times
   b. Ten times

7. Can a fly see in more directions at one time than a human being?
   a. Yes
   b. No

8. What kind of food do flies eat?
   a. Any food
   b. Liquid food

9. How do insects breathe?
   a. Through their mouths
   b. Through their bellies

10. Do fleas have wings?
    a. Yes
    b. No

Video Activity • Natural Disasters in Japan

1. One type of natural disaster is the earthquake. What are some others? Which ones sometimes occur in Japan? Review these terms: *simulation exercise, seismically active.*

2. As you watch the video, listen for the information you need to answer the following questions. The first one is done.

   a. What natural disaster happened about 70 years ago in Japan?
      <u>An earthquake</u>

   b. How many people were killed in the earthquake?

      _____

   c. What happens each year on the anniversary of the earthquake?

      _____

   d. List four other types of natural disasters that sometimes occur in Japan.

      _____

3. After you watch the video, check your answers. Discuss what other things we can do to save lives in a natural disaster.

Internet Activity

Choose one of the following types of disasters: flood, hurricane, or earthquake. Go to the Internet to find out what emergency measures you should follow if such a disaster happens. Make a list of the most important points to remember and why they are important.

Inventions

CHAPTER ELEVEN

Corn Flakes

Pre-Reading Activity

Discuss these questions.

1. What do you eat for breakfast?
2. Do you like cereal? If so, what kind?
3. Why do people eat cereal in the morning?

Key Vocabulary

Do you know these words? Match the words with the meanings.

1. ＿＿ patient   a. old; not fresh
2. ＿＿ stale   b. try new things
3. ＿＿ roll   c. sick person who is under the care of a doctor
4. ＿＿ cereal   d. use words to show that you don't agree
5. ＿＿ serve   e. turn a rounded object over and over on something to make it smooth
6. ＿＿ argue
7. ＿＿ experiment   f. a breakfast food made of grain

     g. give people something, such as food at a meal

Corn Flakes

Will Kellogg was born in 1860. He had no idea that one day he would change the way we eat breakfast. Will had little education compared to his brother John Kellogg. John was the chief doctor at the Battle Creek Health Center in Michigan, where mostly rich people went to eat healthy food and recover their health. Will worked very hard at his brother's health center. He was the accountant and manager and did everything else his brother didn't want to do. He also helped John look for new healthy foods for his **patients.** They worked together, trying to make a new healthy bread for breakfast from wheat. They tried everything with the wheat; they boiled it and then **rolled** it out flat, but nothing seemed to work.

One day, Will cooked some wheat, as usual, and then had to leave. When he returned, the wheat had become **stale.** He decided to put this wheat through rollers anyway. To his surprise, each grain of wheat came out as a flake. When he **baked** the flakes in the oven to get them dry, they became light brown in color. After he tried this a few times, he produced wheat flakes without the stale wheat. He asked his brother John to **serve** the new breakfast food in the dining room of the health center. The patients ate the new breakfast food and loved it. It was 1894, and a new **cereal** was born.

Even after they left the health center, patients ordered bags of the cereal. By 1895, John and Will were producing 100,000 pounds of flakes every year and selling each ten-ounce box for fifteen cents. John was not interested in taking care of this new food business and left all the work to his brother, as usual. Will continued to **experiment** with new foods for the next few years and came out with a new cereal made from corn—he called it corn flakes!

One of the patients at the health center was a man named Charles Post. As he walked around the health center, he watched how the cereal was made. When he returned home, he started his own cereal company. By 1900, the Post Cereal Company was making $3 million in sales. About this time, more than twenty other breakfast companies started in Battle Creek—all making cereals. The Kellogg brothers were angry that other people were using their ideas and getting rich.

The two brothers started to **argue** about the future of their cereal. John wanted it to be part of his health center only, while Will wanted to start a cereal company. This argument turned brother against brother, and they stopped working together. In 1906, Will opened his own cereal company, called the Toasted Corn Flake Company, and started to sell corn flakes. By 1907, his company was producing 2,900 cases of cereal every day. Will increased sales of his cereal all the time, spending millions on advertising.

Will Kellogg and his son worked together in the company. But they argued a lot, and in the end Will told his son to leave. By 1948, the Kellogg Company had sales of more than $100 million. Will Kellogg made millions of dollars, but he continued to live a simple life. He lived in a simple two-story house and preferred to give most of his money to help others, especially children. In 1930, Will Kellogg had started the Kellogg Foundation to help children. Will Kellogg died in 1951, at the age of ninety-one. He worked until the end of his life at the foundation. His company had become the world's largest producer of ready-to-eat cereal as the result of an accident. People continue to eat cereals because all they need is a bowl, a spoon, some milk, and a box of cereal.

Vocabulary

Meaning

Complete the sentences with the following words.

cereal	argued	stale	experimented
patients	served	rolled	

1. The people who went to the health center were ＿＿＿＿＿ of Dr. John Kellogg.

2. To make the boiled wheat into a flat sheet, John and Will Kellogg ＿＿＿＿＿ it.

3. At the health center, Dr. Kellogg ＿＿＿＿＿ healthy food.

4. Will tried different things with the wheat; he ＿＿＿＿＿.

5. Will baked the flakes to make his new ＿＿＿＿＿.

6. Will left the wheat for a long time, and it became _____.

7. The brothers did not agree; they _____.

Vocabulary Activity

Answer the questions. Use complete sentences.

1. What kind of cereal do you like?

   _____

2. What does stale bread look like?

   _____

3. What do they serve for breakfast in hotels in your country?

   _____

4. With whom do you usually argue?

   _____

5. What things do you experiment with?

   _____

6. What is something that you could roll?

   _____

Comprehension

Looking for the Main Ideas

Circle the letter of the best answer.

1. Will Kellogg _____.
   a. found a new breakfast food by accident
   b. and his brother found a new cereal
   c. found a new way to make bread
   d. was a doctor

2. Will Kellogg ——————.

    a. worked with Charles Post

    b. started his own cereal company

    c. and his brother started a cereal company

    d. invented wheat flakes

3. Will Kellogg ——————.

    a. did not like children

    b. lived like a millionaire

    c. gave a lot of his money to help children

    d. lived in a mansion

Looking for Details

Answer the questions with complete sentences.

1. Where did Will Kellogg work?

    _____

2. What did Will cook to make the new cereal?

    _____

3. Who was Charles Post?

    _____

4. What did Charles Post do after he left the health center?

    _____

5. When did Will Kellogg start his own cereal company?

    _____

6. What did the Kellogg Foundation do?

    _____

Discussion

1. Why do people invent things?
2. What is your favorite invention? Why is it useful?
3. Make a list of some inventions you use.

Read the following paragraph written by a student.

Model Paragraph

My Answering Machine

I got an answering machine for my birthday, and I soon realized what a useful machine this is. I am not home most of the day, so someone can leave a message and I can call back. There is no way people can say they can't get in touch with you. Sometimes when I am home and have work to do, the phone never stops. Now I put the machine on. I am not disturbed; therefore, I can do more work. There are some people I just do not want to talk to. Therefore, I put the machine on, and I don't have to speak to them. In conclusion, I really do not know how I lived without this wonderful invention.

Organizing

Cause and Effect Paragraph

In Unit Five, we looked at the word **because**, which introduces the reason for or cause of something. In this lesson, we will look at the effect of something.

First, you must see the difference between the *cause* and the *effect*. The following examples show the cause and the effect. Notice that an effect can have several causes.

Examples:

1. Mary was late for work. **(Effect)**
    She said her alarm clock does not work. **(Cause)**

2.   This machine does not work. **(Effect)**
     It is not plugged in. **(Cause)**

3.   There are no computers in our school. **(Effect)**
     The school does not have money to buy them. **(Cause)**
     There is no room to put them in the school. **(Cause)**
     Most of our teachers do not like computers. **(Cause)**

Exercise 1

Say which statement is the cause and which is the effect.

1.   This light is out.   *effect*
     There is no light bulb.   *cause*

2.   The telephone does not work.   _____
     The storm last night pulled the lines down.   _____

3.   I forgot to put batteries in it.   _____
     My portable radio does not work.   _____

4.   The flight from Canada is three hours late.   _____
     There is a snowstorm in Canada.   _____

5.   I cannot see well with these old glasses.   _____
     I need to have my eyes tested again.   _____

6.   The printer needs a new cartridge.   _____
     There is no writing when I print out.   _____

Using *so* and *therefore*

Look at the model paragraph. Underline the words **so** and **therefore**. Both of these words introduce effect clauses. Now look at the punctuation used with these words. Circle the punctuation before and after these words.

Example:

I am not disturbed { **, so** / **; therefore,** / **. Therefore,** } I can do more work.

So and **therefore** have the same meaning, but **therefore** is more formal.

Exercise 2

Punctuate these sentences with a comma where necessary.

1. Mr. Jones has a hearing problem; therefore he wears a hearing aid.

2. Janet does not like to wear her glasses so she is wearing contact lenses.

3. Peter bought an expensive car. Therefore he had to get a car alarm.

4. John got a photocopier for his office so he does not have to rush to the copy store every day.

5. Kathy always has her answering machine on; therefore you can leave a message tonight.

6. Tony hates to wash dishes so he bought a dishwasher.

Exercise 3

Choose the best clause for the list below to complete each sentence.

I am not home during the day
My alarm clock does not work
Typing is not so important for most office jobs today
His phone is out of order
I studied in the language lab all last semester
My eyesight is not so good in the dark

1. _____ ;

therefore, there is a busy signal on his phone all the time.

2. _____ ,

so I got up late.

3. _____ .

Therefore, I drive very carefully at night.

4. _____ ,

so I leave my answering machine on.

5. _____ ;

therefore, I am learning to use a computer.

6. _____ .

Therefore, my English pronunciation is much better.

Exercise 4

Find the mistakes. There are 10 mistakes in grammar, punctuation, capitalization, and spelling. Find and correct them.

Will Kellogg is born in Battle Creek Michigan, on april 7 1860. He died on October 6 1951. Kellogg was ninety-one year old, when he died. He created corn flakes. Other companies made cereals two. Therefore he called his cereal Kellogg's Corn Flakes.

Writing Practice

Choose one of the topics below:
1. A great invention (microwave oven, fax machine, etc.)
2. An object that I want to invent
3. An invention that I don't like

1. Pre-writing.

        Work with a group, a partner, or alone.

    a.   Write your topic at the top of your paper.

    b.   Think of as many causes and effects about the topic as you can. Write down every word or phrase that comes into your mind about the topic.

    c.   Write your ideas in any order you like. Don't worry about whether or not the idea is important. Write it down.

2. Develop an outline.

    a.   Organize your ideas.

        Step 1: Write the main idea sentence.

        Step 2: Pick three of the best causes and effects from the ones you wrote.

        Step 3: Remember to use the words **so** and **therefore.**

    b.   Make a more detailed outline. The paragraph outline below will help you.

Paragraph Outline

(Topic sentence)	_____ .
(Cause 1)	_____ ,
(Effect)	so _____ .
(Cause 2)	_____ .
(Effect)	Therefore, _____ .
(Cause 3)	_____ ;
(Effect)	therefore, _____ .
(Concluding sentence)	_____ .

3. Write a rough draft.

4. Revise your rough draft.

Using the checklist below, check your rough draft or let your partner check it.

Paragraph Checklist

____ Did you give your paragraph a title?
____ Did you indent the first line?
____ Did you write on every other line?
____ Does your paragraph have a topic sentence?
____ Does your topic sentence have a controlling idea?
____ Do your other sentences support your topic sentence?
____ Are your ideas in the correct order?
____ Does your paragraph have a concluding sentence?

5. Edit your paragraph.

Work with a partner or your teacher to edit your paragraph. Check spelling, punctuation, vocabulary, and grammar.

6. Write your final copy.

CHAPTER TWELVE

Robots

Pre-Reading Activity

Discuss these questions.

1. What kinds of things would you like to have a robot do for you?
2. In what ways are people using robots today?
3. How can a robot be useful in a school?

Key Vocabulary

Do you know these words? Match the words with the meanings.

1. _____ smart
2. _____ enter
3. _____ flexible
4. _____ switch off
5. _____ create
6. _____ emotions
7. _____ mood
8. _____ pay attention

a. look and listen carefully
b. bring into existence
c. the general way you feel
d. intelligent
e. feelings
f. able to change easily
g. stop something electric by pushing a button or moving a bar
h. push buttons to give a word or number

Robots

Robots are **smart.** With their computer brains, they can do work that humans prefer not to do because it is dangerous, dirty, or boring. Some robots are taking jobs away from people. Bobby is a mail carrier robot that brings mail to a large office building in Washington, D.C. There are hundreds of mail carrier robots in the United States. In more than seventy hospitals around the world, robots called Help Mates take medicine down halls, call for elevators, and deliver meals. In Washington, D.C., a tour guide at the Smithsonian museum is a robot called Minerva. About 20 percent of the people who met Minerva said that she seemed as intelligent as a person. There is even a robot that is a teacher.

Mr. Leachim is a fourth-grade teacher robot. He weighs 200 pounds, is six feet tall, and has some advantages as a teacher. One advantage is that he doesn't forget details. He knows each child's name, the parents' names, and what each child knows and needs to know. In addition, he knows each child's pets and hobbies. Mr. Leachim doesn't make mistakes. Each child tells Mr. Leachim his or her name and then **enters** an identification number. His computer brain puts the child's voice and number together. He identifies the child with no mistakes. Then he starts the lesson.

Another advantage is that Mr. Leachim is **flexible.** If the children do not understand something, they can repeat Mr. Leachim's lesson over and over again. When the children do a good job, he tells them something interesting about their hobbies. At the end of the lesson, the children **switch off** Mr. Leachim. The good thing about Mr. Leachim is that he doesn't have a nervous system like a human, so he doesn't get upset if a child is "difficult."

Today, scientists are trying to **create** a robot that shows **emotions** like a human being. At M.I.T. (Massachusetts Institute of Technology), Cynthia Breazeal has created a robot called Kismet. It has only a head at this time. As soon as Breazeal comes and sits in front of Kismet, the robot's **mood** changes. The robot smiles. Breazeal talks to it the way a mother talks to a child, and Kismet watches and smiles. When Breazeal starts to move backward and forward, Kismet doesn't like that and looks upset. The message Kismet is giving is "Stop this!" Breazeal stops, and Kismet becomes calm. Breazeal now **pays** no **attention** to Kismet, and the robot becomes sad. When Breazeal turns toward Kismet, the robot is happy again. Another thing Kismet does like a child is to play with a toy and then become bored with the toy and close its eyes and go to sleep. Breazeal is still developing Kismet. Kismet still has many things missing in its personality. It does not have all human emotions yet, but one day it will!

At one time, people said that computers could not have emotions. It looks very possible that in the future scientists will develop a computer that does have emotions and can even be a friend. But what are the advantages of having a friend that's a machine?

Vocabulary

Meaning

Complete the sentences with the following words.

enters	pay attention
create	mood
flexible	switch off
emotions	smart

1. Robots with their computer brains are _____ .

2. Cynthia Breazeal is trying to _____ a robot that has feelings.

3. Kismet does not have _____ like love.

4. When a person looks at Kismet for the first time, the robot's _____ changes.

5. Kismet doesn't like it when you don't _____ .

6. A child goes to Mr. Leachim and _____ an identification number.

7. When a child needs more time or needs Mr. Leachim to repeat something, the robot is _____ .

8. When the lesson finishes, the child can _____ Mr. Leachim.

Vocabulary Activity

Answer the questions. Use complete sentences.

1. Who is a smart student in your class?

   _____

2. When do you enter a number?

   _____

3. To whom do you usually pay attention in class?

   _____

4. What machine do you switch on and off?

   _____

5. What emotion do you feel when you do well on a test?

   _____

6. What mood are you in most of the time?

   _____

7. What can you create with a piece of paper?

   _____

Comprehension

Looking for the Main Ideas

Circle the letter of the best answer.

1. Robots _____.
   a. can help people in regular jobs
   b. cannot help people do difficult jobs
   c. work only in hospitals
   d. work only in post offices

2. Mr. Leachim is a _____
   a. mail carrier robot
   b. fourth-grade teacher
   c. fourth-grade teacher robot
   d. Help Mate robot

3. Kismet is a_____.
   a. dog robot
   b. robot that has some emotions
   c. robot that is just like a human
   d. Help Mate robot

Looking for Details

Circle T if the sentence is true. Circle F if the sentence is false.

1.	Bobby is a mail carrier robot in an office building.	T F
2.	Hospitals use robots called Help Mates.	T F
3.	Mr. Leachim identifies a child by his or her voice only.	T F
4.	When the lesson is over, the child enters an identification number.	T F
5.	Kismet cries when it doesn't like something.	T F
6.	Kismet goes to sleep when it is bored.	T F

Discussion

Discuss these questions with your classmates.
1. Discuss what you want robots to do in the future.
2. List four advantages (good things) and four disadvantages (bad things) of having a robot teacher.

Read the following paragraph written by a student.

Model Paragraph

A Robot Teacher

In my opinion, you get some advantages if you have a robot to teach you English. First of all, you feel at ease and relaxed. When you make a mistake, you are not embarrassed. Second, the student is in control. You can ask the robot to repeat something over and over again, but you cannot ask your teacher to do that. In addition, learning with a robot is like a game. It is fun. Learning with a teacher is usually not like a game. In conclusion, a robot teacher makes you feel at ease and in control, and you have fun.

Organizing

Advantages and Disadvantages

The paragraph above tells us the advantages (the good sides) of something. It is organized in this way. First is the topic sentence. Then comes the advantage, starting with

> **First of all, . . .**
> or
> **First, . . .**
> or
> **The first advantage is** . . .

and followed by a supporting sentence.

Then comes the next advantage, starting with

Second, . . .

or

The second advantage is . . .

and followed by a supporting sentence.

Any other advantages also start with

In addition, . . .

or

Moreover, . . .

and are followed by a supporting sentence.

At the end is

In conclusion, . . .

Read the model paragraph again. How many advantages are there?

Fact or Opinion?

Now look at the topic sentence of the model paragraph. The student gives us a statement of opinion. It is not a fact. A statement of fact gives information that everyone thinks is true. An opinion tells us what one person thinks is true. Other people may have different opinions.

Exercise 1

Are the statements below facts or opinions? Circle the correct answer.

1. You fell at ease and relaxed with a robot teacher.

    Fact   Opinion

2. There are some 250 mail carrier robots in the United States.

    Fact   Opinion

3. With a robot teacher the student is in control.

    Fact   Opinion

4. Mr. Leachim, the robot teacher, weighs 200 pounds and is six feet tall.

   Fact   Opinion

5. Learning with a robot is like a game.

   Fact   Opinion

If your statement is an opinion, you can start with one of the following:

In my opinion, . . .
I believe . . .
I think . . .
I feel . . .

After you give an opinion, you must support it with facts and/or examples.

Transitions Showing Addition: in addition and moreover

When you give a list of advantages, reasons, or other ideas in a paragraph, you can use transitions that show addition. Transitions like **in addition** and **moreover** show addition. **In addition** and **moreover** have the same meaning.

First (of all), . . .
Second, . . .
In addition, . . .
Moreover, . . .
Finally, . . .

In addition and **moreover** are not always placed at the beginning of the sentence. Look at the examples below and note the punctuation used with each.

Examples:

In addition, he know each child's pets and hobbies.
He knows, **in addition,** each child's pets and hobbies.

Moreover, he knows each child's pet and hobbies.
He knows, **moreover,** each child's pets and hobbies.

Now underline the transition that shows addition in the model paragraph. Circle the punctuation marks before and after the transition words.

In the sentences below, **in addition** and **moreover** are used in the middle of sentences. Rewrite the sentences. Put the words **in addition** and **moreover** at the beginning of the sentences. Use the correct punctuation.

1. The robot CORA was a brain on wheels. CORA, in addition, could recharge her own batteries.

   _____

   _____

2. The Brave Cop robot can disarm bombs. Brave Cop, moreover, can shoot his gun.

   _____

   _____

3. The Security Guard robot finds the enemy with his special sensors. The Security Guard, in addition, uses high sounds to hurt the enemy.

   _____

   _____

4. DA II, the Robot Maid, can do all kinds of jobs in the house. DA II, moreover, can do jobs in the yard.

   _____

   _____

5. The robot AROK can do many things in the home, like vacuum, take out the trash, and bring in the mail. AROK, in addition, can tell jokes.

_____

_____

6. Beetle, the Robot Truck, can break down walls. Beetle, moreover, can be very gentle.

_____

_____

Find the mistakes. There are 10 mistakes in grammar, punctuation, and capitalization. Find and correct them.

A new Robot vacuum cleaner can clean the house so we can have more time for ourselves. The Robot was created by Rodney Brooks at M.I.T., in Boston Massachusetts. The robot is named Roomba. When it moves through the house it avoids anything that is in front of it. When it comes to stairs it turns away from them. The Robot adapts to different floors with, or without carpet. The Roomba costs about two hundreds U.S. Dollars.

Writing Practice

Choose one of the topics below:

1. The disadvantages of a robot teacher
2. The advantages or disadvantages of a robot security guard
3. The advantages or disadvantages of a robot astronaut

1. **Pre-writing.**

   Work with a group, a partner, or alone.

   a. Write your topic at the top of your paper.
   b. Think of as many reasons to support your opinion as possible. Remember to choose only one side: advantages or disadvantages.
   c. Which of these reasons can you support with facts or examples?

2. **Develop an outline.**

   a. Organize your ideas.

   Step 1: Write the topic sentence, which tells the reader your position on the subject (Advantages/Disadvantages of . . .). If it is an opinion, use the words "In my opinion, . . ." or "I believe . . ." or something similar.

   Step 2: Pick three supporting reasons for your opinion. Make sure that these reasons are different from each other and that you can write a supporting sentence (with a fact or personal example) for each.

   Step 3: Remember to introduce each reason.

   b. Make a more detailed outline. The paragraph outline on the next page will help you.

Paragraph Outline

(Topic sentence) _____ .

(First advantage/ disadvantage) _____ .

(Supporting sentence) _____ .

(Second advantage/ disadvantage) _____ .

(Supporting sentence) _____ .

(Third advantage/ disadvantage) In addition, _____ .

(Supporting sentence) _____ .

(Concluding sentence) _____ .

3. Write a rough draft.

4. Revise your rough draft.

> Using the checklist below, check your rough draft or let your partner check it.

> **Paragraph Checklist**
> _____ Did you give your paragraph a title?
> _____ Did you indent the first line?
> _____ Did you write on every other line?
> _____ Does your paragraph have a topic sentence?
> _____ Does your topic sentence have a controlling idea?
> _____ Do your reasons support your topic sentence?
> _____ Are your ideas in the correct order?
> _____ Does your paragraph have a concluding sentence?

5. Edit your paragraph.

> Work with a partner or your teacher to edit your paragraph. Check spelling, punctuation, vocabulary, and grammar.

6. Write your final copy.

Inventions quiz

Circle the correct answer.

1. Who invented the electric light bulb?

   a. Thomas Alva Edison   b. Albert Einstein   c. Marie Curie

2. A thermos bottle keeps hot drinks hot and cold drinks cold. The word thermos is Greek. It means —————.

   a. hot   b. cold   c. temperature

3. In 1876, Alexander Graham Bell said to his assistant, "Watson, come here. I want you." What was his invention?

   a. Telegraph   b. Television   c. Telephone

4. Alexander Fleming discovered penicillin in 1929. What nationality was he?

   a. German   b. Scottish   c. American

5. We named a popular food after this person. He loved to play cards. One day, he got hungry but did not want to leave the card game. He told his servants to bring him some meat between two slices of bread. He was the Earl of —————.

   a. Hamburger   b. Deli   c. Sandwich

6. A kind of stove and bifocal eyeglasses were the inventions of a famous American statesman. Who was he?

   a. George Washington   b. Benjamin Franklin   c. Abraham Lincoln

7. John Baird (1888–1946) was a Scottish inventor. What was his famous invention?

   a. Television   b. Color photography   c. Vacuum cleaner

8. The Nobel Prize, a special prize for people who work for peace in the world, is named after Alfred Nobel. Alfred Nobel invented —————.

   a. radium   b. radar   c. dynamite

Video Activity • Robodog

1. The video describes a robot called Robodog. Do you think people will have robots in their homes in the future? Will they be like pets, or will they do some work in the home, or both? Discuss these expressions from the video that refer to dogs: *man's best friend, retrieve, pet project, canine, mutt, pup, Labrador, "Every dog will have its day."*

2. Read the following statements. Then, as you watch the video, listen for the information you need to decide whether they are true or false.

   a. Robodog talks, does tricks, and vacuums the carpet. <u>False</u>

   b. Robodog weighs about 20 kilos. ____

   c. Since Robodog contains a camera, it can be used as a guard dog. ____

   d. Robodog took a little over a year to make. ____

   e. Although Robodog can be used in the home, the manufacturers hope it will also have commercial and military uses. ____

3. After you watch the video, fill in your answers. Remember that if any part of the statement is incorrect, the statement is false. The first one is done.

4. Would you like to have a robot like Robodog? What are some ways you would use it besides the ones described in the video?

Internet Activity

Think of a modern invention that you use every day. Here are some ideas: the vacuum cleaner, the telephone, teabags, peanut butter. Then go to the Internet to find out who invented it and when. Find out as much as you can about how it was invented. Write a summary of the story of the invention and the effects of the invention.

The Law

CHAPTER THIRTEEN

It's the Law

Pre-Reading Activity

Discuss these questions.

1. Do you think that there are too many laws?
2. What do you think is an example of a bad law in North America? Give your reasons.
3. What do you think is a very good law? Give your reasons.

Key Vocabulary

Do you know these words? Match the words with the meanings.

1. ____ federal
2. ____ layer
3. ____ strict
4. ____ get arrested
5. ____ helmet
6. ____ county
7. ____ license
8. ____ unattended

a. severe
b. get caught and kept by the police for doing something wrong
c. something that lies under or on top of something else
d. of the central government
e. permit from the government to do something
f. area within a state
g. protective head covering
h. alone; not watched

It's the law, but which law—**federal** or state law? In the United States, there are different **layers** of laws. At the top is federal law, which Congress makes for all people in the United States. Then each state makes laws about things in its territory. The laws that each state makes must not go against federal laws. **Counties** and towns also make rules. A town may require that you have a **license** for your bicycle, for example. Here are some similarities and differences in state laws.

The ages for going to school and for getting a driver's license differ from state to state. In California, children must go to school from age seven to age sixteen. However, in the state of Oregon, they must go from age seven to age eighteen. Similarly, there are differences in when you get your driver's license. In California, you can get a regular driver's license without driver's education at age eighteen, and you can get one with driver's education at age sixteen. However, in Louisiana, you can get a school instruction permit to drive at age fourteen!

Some countries, like Australia, France, and Germany, have laws about wearing **helmets** when driving a motorcycle. However, there is no federal law in the United States about this. Twenty states have helmet laws for all riders, and twenty-seven states have laws covering some riders, usually those younger than eighteen. However, states like Colorado, Illinois, and Iowa have no helmet laws. Likewise, there is no federal law about bicycle helmets in the United States; however, states have started to make their own laws. For example, in California, riders under the age of eighteen must wear helmets. Whereas in Hawaii, Maine, and Georgia, the age is sixteen, and in Massachusetts, it is thirteen!

There is no federal law about leaving children **unattended** in cars. However, eleven states have **strict** laws about leaving young children alone, either in cars, in public places, or at home. In those states, it is against the law to leave anyone in a car who cannot get out without help. Sometimes, when a child is sleeping in the car and the parent doesn't want to wake the child up, the parent might decide to leave the child in the car and go into the store to get something. The parent can

get arrested for this. Similarly, it is against the law to leave a child alone at home or outside a public place like a restaurant. However, some states, like California, Hawaii, and Massachusetts, don't have any laws as yet about leaving children unattended in cars.

Capital punishment (the death penalty) for serious crimes is a subject people always argue about. Most European countries do not have the death penalty. However, thirty-eight states in the United States have the death penalty, including California and New York. However, other states, like Hawaii and Alaska, don't have the death penalty.

Some states have a number of very strange old laws. Most people have never heard of these laws. Nobody gets arrested for breaking them, but they are still laws. For example, in Kentucky, everybody must have a bath at least once a year. In Indiana, you cannot travel on a bus less than four hours after you eat garlic. In California, it is against the law to enter a restaurant on horseback.

Vocabulary

Meaning

Complete the sentences with the following words.

federal	get arrested
license	strict
layers	counties
helmet	unattended

1. If you leave your child in a car alone, you can _____ .

2. Many states have laws about wearing a _____ when you ride a motorcycle.

3. _____ , which are parts of a state, also have their own rules.

4. You need a _____ to drive a car.

5. The laws that Congress makes for the whole country are _____ laws.

6. There are many _____ of laws in the United States, with federal laws at the top.

7. Some states have ——————— laws about leaving children alone in a car.

8. If you leave a child alone in a car, the child is ——————— .

Vocabulary Activity

Answer the questions. Use complete sentences.

1. Who do you think is a strict teacher?

    _____

    _____

2. What should you not leave unattended at an airport?

    _____

    _____

3. What do you need a license for?

    _____

    _____

4. Who wears a helmet?

    _____

    _____

5. What is something you put on in layers?

    _____

    _____

Comprehension

Looking for the Main Ideas

Circle the letter of the best answer.

1. In the United States, there _____.
   a. is only one law
   b. are only state laws
   c. are different layers of laws
   d. are only federal laws

2. Each state makes its _____.
   a. own laws
   b. laws for driver's licenses only
   c. laws the same as in California
   d. laws for schools and traffic only

3. Some states have old laws that _____.
   a. everyone gets arrested for
   b. are very strange
   c. are not really laws anymore
   d. are laws from other countries

Looking for Details

Circle T if the sentence is true. Circle F if the sentence is false.

1. In California, children must go to school until they are eighteen.   T   F

2. In Colorado, you can drive a motorcycle without a helmet.   T   F

3. Twenty-eight states have the death penalty.   T   F

4. In California, you must wear a bicycle helmet if you are under the age of fourteen.   T   F

5. You cannot leave a child unattended in a car in Hawaii.   T   F

6. In Kentucky, you must have a bath at least once a year.   T   F

Discussion

Discuss these questions with your classmates.

1. At what age can you get a driver's license in your country? How long must you attend school?

2. Which laws in your country do you think should be changed?

3. Do you know any strange laws in your country or in another country?

4. Discuss the rules and regulations of the school you went to in your country. Then list three things that are different in your present school. List three things that are the same.

Now read the following paragraph written by a student. What country does the student come from?

Model Paragraph

Classroom Behavior Rules

There are some similarities and differences in the classroom behavior rules between North America and my country. First, there is the student's right to speak. In my language class in North America, students can ask the teacher questions. They can even ask questions when the teacher is giving a lesson. Similarly, in my country, students have the right to ask questions. However, they can ask questions only at the end of the class. Next, students respect their teachers. In North America, students look up to teachers and respect them. For example, when the teacher asks them to speak, they must look into the teacher's eyes to show respect. Likewise, in my country, students respect teachers; however, when a teacher asks us to speak, we look down to show respect. We do not look into the teacher's eyes. In conclusion, there are both similarities and differences in the way students behave toward their teachers in the classroom.

Organizing

Comparing and Contrasting

In this unit, you will learn how to organize a compare-and-contrast paragraph.

When we *compare,* we look at the similarities between two things, two people, two ideas, etc. When we *contrast,* we look at the differences.

There are two ways of organizing your paragraph when you compare and contrast. Plan A and Plan B are outlines of the two ways you can organize your compare-and-contrast paragraph.

Look at the outlines and then look at the model paragraph just given. Which outline does it follow—Plan A or Plan B? How many similarities can you see in the model paragraph? How many differences can you see in the model paragraph?

Plan A

Topic sentence

  I. Similarities: North America and my country
      A. The right to speak
      B. Respect for teacher
 II. Differences: North America and my country
      A. The right to speak
      B. Respect for teacher

Concluding sentence

Plan B

Topic sentence

  I. The right to speak
      A. Similarities: North America and my country
      B. Differences: North America and my country
 II. Respect for teacher
      A. Similarities: North America and my country
      B. Differences: North America and my country

Concluding sentence

Transitions Showing Contrast: *however*

However connects an idea in the first sentence with a contrasting idea in the second sentence. **However** tells the reader that an idea opposite from the one in the first sentence will follow. **However** has the same meaning as **but**. **However** is used mostly in formal writing. Notice the punctuation used with **however**. Both of the following examples have the same meaning.

Examples:

In California, children go to school until age sixteen; **however**, in Oregon, they go to school until age eighteen.

In California, children go to school until age sixteen. **However**, in Oregon, they go to school until age eighteen.

Now underline the transition **however** in the reading passage and in the model paragraph.Next, look at the punctuation with **however.** Go back and circle all the punctuation marks with **however.**

Exercise 1

Connect the following sentences with **however.** Use **however** with both kinds of punctuation.

1. In California, you can get a driver's license at age eighteen. In Colorado, you must be twenty-one.

    _____

    _____

2. In the United States, students in high school do not wear uniforms. In my country, students must wear uniforms.

    _____

    _____

3. In most countries, people drive on the right. In Great Britain and Australia, people drive on the left.

    _____

    _____

4. In North America, letter grades are given in high school. In my country, numbers 1 to 10 are given.

    _____

    _____

Transitions Showing Similarity: *similarly* and *likewise*

The transitions **similarly** and **likewise** connect an idea in the first sentence with a similar idea in the second sentence. **Similarly** or **likewise** introduces the second sentence. Use a comma after **similarly** or **likewise.**

Example:

In North America, students can ask the teacher questions.
Likewise,
Similarly, } in my country, students have the right to ask the teacher questions.

Connect the following sentences with **similarly** or **likewise.** Use the correct punctuation.

1. Students in the United States respect their teachers. In my country, students respect their teachers.

   _____

   _____

2. In California, you must attend school until age sixteen. In Alaska, Colorado, Arizona, and Florida, you must attend school until you are sixteen.

   _____

   _____

3. A driver in a car must wear a seat belt. The passenger sitting next to the driver must wear a seat belt.

   _____

   _____

4. You may not vote until you are eighteen. Before you are eighteen, you cannot write a will or make a contract.

   _____

   _____

Exercise 3

Find the mistakes. There are 10 mistakes in grammar, punctuation, and capitalization. Find and correct them.

In most States in the United States the speed limit is 65 miles an hour on a freeway, unless it is marked differently. In arizona, the speed limit is 85. In Colorado it is 75. It is against law to drive over speed limit. However in some States going over the limit by 5 miles is acceptable. In other States, driving 10 or 15 miles over the limit is acceptable.

Writing Practice

Choose one of the topics below to compare and contrast:

1. Traffic laws/regulations in your country and in North America (or another country)
2. Past and present class/school rules
3. Police officers in your country and in North America (or another country)

1. Pre-writing.

Work with a group, a partner, or alone.

a. Write your topic at the top of your paper.
b. Think of as many similarities as you can. Write them down.
c. Think of as many differences as you can. Write them down.

2. Develop an outline.

a. Organize your ideas.
   Step 1: Write your topic sentence.

   Example:

   There are some interesting similarities and differences in traffic laws between North America and my country, X.

   Step 2: Name two things that make them similar. Then name two things that make them different.
   Step 3: Can you write at least one supporting sentence for each of the similarities and differences above? If you can't find good examples, you may have to change your points.
   Step 4: Remember the compare-and-contrast transitions: **however, likewise, similarly.** Think of where you can put these in your paragraph.

b. Make a more detailed outline. The paragraph outline on the next page will help you.

Paragraph Outline

(Topic sentence) _____ .

(Similarity 1)
(Supporting sentence) _____ .

_____ .

(Similarity 2)
(Supporting sentence) _____ .

_____ .

(Difference 1)
(Supporting sentence) _____ .

_____ .

(Difference 2)
(Supporting sentence) _____ .

(Concluding sentence) _____ .

_____ .

3. Write a rough draft.

4. Revise your rough draft.

> Using the checklist below, check your rough draft or let your partner check it.

> **Paragraph Checklist**
> _____ Did you give your paragraph a title?
> _____ Did you indent the first line?
> _____ Did you write on every other line?
> _____ Does your paragraph have a topic sentence?
> _____ Does your topic sentence have a controlling idea?
> _____ Do your similarities and differences support your topic sentence?
> _____ Are your ideas in the correct order?
> _____ Does your paragraph have a concluding sentence?

5. Edit your paragraph.

> Work with a partner or your teacher to edit your paragraph. Check spelling, punctuation, vocabulary, and grammar.

6. Write your final copy.

CHAPTER FOURTEEN

Laws About Children

Pre-Reading Activity

Discuss these questions.

1. Do you think these children are happy?
2. Do you think such children could work in a factory today?
3. What laws do you know about work by children?

Key Vocabulary

Do you know these words? Match the words with the meanings.

1. _____ beat   a. correct and right
2. _____ punish   b. laugh at
3. _____ make fun of   c. hit again and again
4. _____ fair   d. do not allow; make it against the rules
5. _____ forbid   e. pay money for doing something wrong
6. _____ excuse   f. free; not controlled by anyone
7. _____ pay a fine   g. reason
8. _____ independent   h. make someone feel pain for doing something wrong

Laws About Children

In general, laws about children are a good thing. One hundred years ago in industrial countries, children worked eighteen hours a day in a factory at age seven. The factory owner could **beat** a child who fell asleep or was not fast enough. Both parents and teachers could do whatever they liked to children because children had no protection under the law.

Today, there are many laws to protect children all over the world. Some people think that children must obey rules or be **punished.** Other people do not agree. The Inuit, or Eskimos, in Alaska almost never hit their children. If the children don't obey, the parents **make fun of** them.

Children in the United States are not as lucky as Inuit children. Parents can spank their children at home. Similarly, schools can punish children by spanking or hitting as long as it is "reasonable." There are rules about what is reasonable. These rules look at the child's age, the child's past behavior, why the person is hitting the child, and so on. However, the law says that officials cannot hit people in prisons or mental hospitals in the United States. Some people think it is not **fair** that officials can hit schoolchildren and not prisoners. Many school districts have their own laws and rules that **forbid** hitting students. These laws change from state to state. It really depends on where you live in the United States. In contrast, in Sweden, it is against the law for anyone—parent or teacher—to hit a child.

In the United States, all children must go to school until the age of sixteen. However, in some states, like Hawaii, Utah, and Washington, children must attend school until the age of eighteen! A child cannot miss school without an acceptable **excuse.** There are laws about this. Illness, a death in the family, or an emergency is an acceptable excuse for missing a class or a whole day. Schools are very serious about school attendance. There are laws that make the parents accountable if their children miss school. Parents can go to jail or **pay a fine.** In Colorado, a fifteen-year-old girl went to jail for a month because she missed forty-three days of school and was late nineteen times. Her parents also went to jail for ten days and paid a fine of $300.

In the United States, all children must attend school, and they have the right to do this for free. All children have the right to go to school; it does not matter what their race, sex, or religion is, whether they are American citizens or illegal residents who speak no English, or whether they are disabled in any way. Children can leave school when they are sixteen, whether or not they graduate, and can continue their education until they are twenty-one or they graduate from high school, whichever comes first. However, children do not have the right to attend any school they choose. The law says they must attend school in the community where they live.

The law says children are adults at age eighteen. In the United States, they can work or live away from home and be **independent.** However, if they want to work before the age of eighteen and are still students, they must not work during school hours. They can work only three hours a day when there is school and not more than forty hours a week when there is no school.

Vocabulary

Meaning

Complete the sentences with the following words.

make fun of	punish
forbid	pay a fine
beat	fair
excuse	independent

1. The Inuit almost never _____ their children.

2. When the children do not obey, Inuit parents _____ their children.

3. Many states have laws that _____ hitting students.

4. If you are sick and have a letter from a doctor, it is a good _____ to miss a day of school.

5. Sometimes, parents _____ or go to jail if they let their children miss school.

6. In the old days, some people used to _____ children for no good reason.

7. The laws let officials hit schoolchildren and not prisoners. Some people think this is not _____.

8. After the age of eighteen, if a person works, lives away from home, and pays for himself or herself, that person is _____.

Vocabulary Activity

Answer the questions. Use complete sentences.

1. What excuse do you usually give when you miss class?

   _____

   _____

2. When do people usually pay a fine?

   _____

   _____

3. What school rule do you think is not fair?

   _____

   _____

4. What did your parents forbid you to do when you were young?

   _____

   _____

5. What food do people beat when they cook?

   _____

   _____

6. What is something children get punished for in school?

   _____

   _____

Comprehension

Looking for the Main Ideas

Circle the letter of the best answer.

1. Laws about children are _____.
    a. not a good idea
    b. only for parents
    c. a good thing
    d. for Americans only

2. In the United States, _____.
    a. parents cannot hit children
    b. parents can hit children
    c. school officials cannot hit children
    d. parents and teachers cannot hit children

3. In the United States, all children must _____.
    a. go to school at least until age eighteen
    b. pay to go to school
    c. graduate from high school
    d. go to school at least until age sixteen

Looking for Details

Circle T if the sentence is true. Circle F if the sentence is false.

1. Children must attend school until age eighteen
    in Hawaii.   T   F

2. Illegal residents in the United States cannot get a free
    education.   T   F

3. In Sweden, parents and teachers cannot hit children.   T   F

4. In the United States, a person is an adult at age
    twenty-one.   T   F

5. In the United States, you cannot go to any school you like for free.   T   F

6. Parents can go to jail if their children miss a lot of school.   T   F

Discussion

Discuss these questions with your classmates.

1. Discuss whether it is good or bad for a parent to hit a child.
2. Do you think that teachers in schools should have the right to hit a child?
3. Many young people want to be independent as soon as they can. What are some responsibilities of being independent? Is it easy or hard to be independent?

Read the following business letter. It is a job application letter.

Model Letter

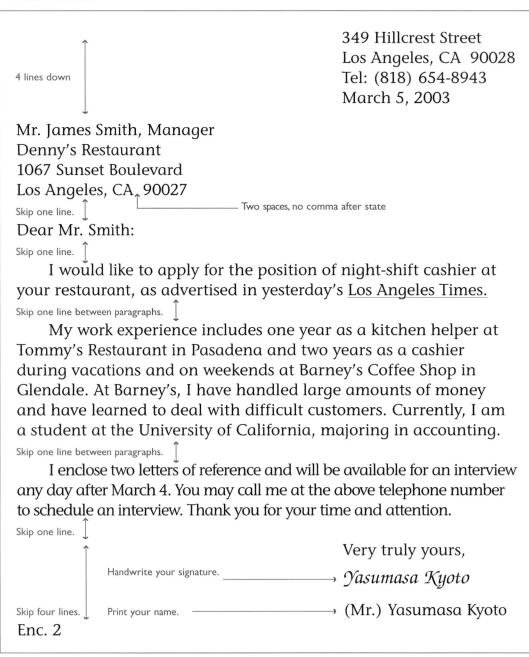

4 lines down

349 Hillcrest Street
Los Angeles, CA 90028
Tel: (818) 654-8943
March 5, 2003

Mr. James Smith, Manager
Denny's Restaurant
1067 Sunset Boulevard
Los Angeles, CA 90027

Two spaces, no comma after state

Skip one line.

Dear Mr. Smith:

Skip one line.

    I would like to apply for the position of night-shift cashier at your restaurant, as advertised in yesterday's <u>Los Angeles Times.</u>

Skip one line between paragraphs.

    My work experience includes one year as a kitchen helper at Tommy's Restaurant in Pasadena and two years as a cashier during vacations and on weekends at Barney's Coffee Shop in Glendale. At Barney's, I have handled large amounts of money and have learned to deal with difficult customers. Currently, I am a student at the University of California, majoring in accounting.

Skip one line between paragraphs.

    I enclose two letters of reference and will be available for an interview any day after March 4. You may call me at the above telephone number to schedule an interview. Thank you for your time and attention.

Skip one line.

Very truly yours,

Handwrite your signature. ⟶ *Yasumasa Kyoto*

Skip four lines.

Print your name. ⟶ (Mr.) Yasumasa Kyoto

Enc. 2

Organizing

Business Letter Form

The writer's address and the date are in the upper right-hand corner of the page. Start the first word in each line at the same place on the line to form a block. Notice the use of commas and periods. Do not use a comma before the ZIP code, which you write two spaces after the state postal abbreviation.

Abbreviations Used in Addresses

Apt.	= Apartment	Ltd.	= Limited
Ave.	= Avenue	No.	= Number
Blvd.	= Boulevard	P.O.	= Post Office
Co.	= Company	Rd.	= Road
Dept.	= Department	St.	= Street
Inc.	= Incorporated		

The receiver's name and address are written on the left, starting four lines down from the date line. Again, start the first word in each line at the same place on the line to form a block.

The *greeting* is written one line down from the last line of the receiver's address. The standard greeting is **Dear (title + name)**. If you do not know the person's name, write **Dear Sir/Madam.** Put a colon (:) after the greeting.

Titles

Mr.	= married or unmarried man
Ms.	= married or unmarried woman
Mrs.	= married woman
Miss	= unmarried woman (no period after Miss because it is not an abbreviation)

The *closing* goes two lines below the body of the letter. It should be in line with the beginning of the writer's address. Capitalize the first word of the closing, and place a comma after it.

Common Closings

Sincerely,
Sincerely yours,
Very truly yours,
Respectfully,
Cordially, (if you know the person you are writing to)

To sign your letter, first type or print your name four lines down from the closing. Your name should start at the same place as your closing. Next, handwrite your signature (in black or dark blue ink) between the closing and your typed name. Note that we write our first names first and family names last. Do not give your title unless your name may be unfamiliar to English speakers and the receiver may not know whether you are a man or woman. In this case, type your title in parentheses before your name.

If you are sending something with your letter, type the word **Enclosure** or its abbreviation, **Encl.,** at the left margin, below your name.

Address the envelope by writing your full name and complete address in the upper left-hand corner of the envelope. Write the receiver's name and address, as in the letter, in the middle of the envelope. Look at this example of an addressed envelope.

Yasumasa Kyoto
349 Hillcrest Street
Los Angeles, CA 90028

Stamp

Mr. James Smith, Manager
Denny's Restaurant
1067 Sunset Boulevard
Los Angeles, CA 90027

Business Letter Content

As a student, you may have to write a business letter to apply for a job or to a school. Or you may need to write a letter to ask for something, such as information about a program in a college. A business letter has three parts, just like a composition. Each part is usually one paragraph. However, in some cases the body may take more than one paragraph.

The following is an outline of a business letter:

Part 1: Introduction   State the purpose of your letter.

Part 2: Body   Give supporting information. (This may take more than one paragraph.)

Part 3: Conclusion   State what you will do or want the reader to do; say thank you.

Now look back at the model letter for a job application.

1.   What is the purpose of the first paragraph?
2.   What information does the second paragraph give? Is this information necessary?
3.   Does the last paragraph ask for or announce an action and give thanks?

Exercise 1

Find the mistakes. There are 10 mistakes in punctuation and capitalization. Find and correct them.

Forty-nine states, and the District of Columbia now have car safety

belt laws. In most States, these laws are for occupants of front seats,

although belt laws in sixteen states, including california new york

and new mexico, are for back seat occupants too.

Writing Practice

Choose *one* of the four topics below and write a short letter requesting the information given in parentheses. Address an envelope with both your name and address and the receiver's name and address. Pay attention to punctuation and capitalization.

1. ms. cheryl browne / director of admissions / university of texas / post office box 220 / dallas / texas / 75208 (Ask for an application form and information about the college. Ask for the TOEFL requirement.)

2. office of admission and records / glendale college / 1500 north verdugo road / glendale / ca / 90028 (Ask that they send a copy of your transcripts to you. Give the semesters and years you attended.)

3. billing inquiries / national bank / post office box 31899 / phoenix / az / 85071 (Ask them to cancel your credit card. Give details.)

4. job application letter / lee's clothing supply store / 246 summer street / boston / ma / 02115 (Apply for a job as a cashier.)

1. Write a rough draft of your letter.

2. Revise and edit your rough draft, using the checklist below.

> **Business Letter Checklist**
> _____ Does your letter have the correct address?
> _____ Does your letter have the correct date?
> _____ Does your letter have an indent for each paragraph?
> _____ Does your letter have the correct spacing between paragraphs?
> _____ Does your letter have correct spelling, punctuation, and grammar?
> _____ Does your letter have your signature and your printed name below it?

3. Write your final copy.

Do you know about these laws?

Are these facts true or false? Circle your answer.

1. In Sweden, you must drive with your car headlights on all the time.   T   F

2. In Germany, there is no law about how fast you can drive on the freeway (Autobahn).   T   F

3. You can be fined $300 if you pick a wildflower anywhere in the United States.   T   F

4. The minimum age for buying alcohol in the United States is twenty.   T   F

5. From all the levels of government—federal, state, and local— Americans get 150 new laws each year.   T   F

6. From all the levels of government—federal, state, and local— Americans get two million new regulations every year.   T   F

7. The age of majority (the age at which a person has legal control over his or her actions) is eighteen in forty-seven of the fifty states in the United States.   T   F

Video Activity • Moles and the Law   CNN

1. The video describes the problem caused by small animals called moles in Washington state, where it is against the law to trap them. Review the following terms used in the video: *mounds, critters, exhaust* (as a noun), *sonic, Juicy Fruit.*

2. As you watch the video, make a list of the methods people have tried to get rid of the moles. You should have a list of five methods. The first is given:

   a. _Chewing gum_____

   b. _____

   c. _____

   d. _____

   e. _____

3. After you watch the video, check your answers. What is the meaning of the phrase "to make a mountain out of a molehill"?

Internet Activity

Choose two different countries. Go to the Internet to find out at what age you can get married, leave school, drive a car, and vote in each of these countries. Write a paragraph comparing the laws in these countries.

Readings from Literature

CHAPTER FIFTEEN

A Poem

Pre-Reading Activity

Discuss these questions.

1. What fruit is in the picture?
2. If you were very hungry, would you eat it?
3. What is your favorite fruit? Why do you like it?

Key Vocabulary

Do you know these words? Match the words with the meanings.

1. —— icebox   a. stop being angry with someone; pardon someone
2. —— forgive   b. keep something for the future
3. —— delicious   c. refrigerator; a place to keep food cold
4. —— save   d. having a good taste

This is Just to Say
by William Carlos Williams

This is Just to Say

I have eaten
the plums
that were in
the **icebox**

and which
you were probably
saving
for breakfast

Forgive me
they were **delicious**
so sweet
and so cold

Vocabulary

Meaning

Complete the sentences with the following words.

forgive	delicious
saving	icebox

1. We put the food in the _____ to keep it cold and fresh.

2. The plums tasted very good. They were _____.

3. I don't want to eat the plums now. I am _____ them for later.

4. I'm sorry that I upset you. Please _____ me.

Answer the questions. Use complete sentences.

1. What fruit do you put in your icebox?

   _____

   _____

2. What is something you like to save?

   _____

   _____

3. What food do you think is delicious?

   _____

   _____

4. What is something you could never forgive?

   _____

   _____

Comprehension

Understanding the Poem

Write complete answers to these questions.

1. Why did the speaker write the poem?

   _____

   _____

2. What did the speaker do that was wrong?

   _____

   _____

3. How does the speaker feel about what he did?

   _____

   _____

4. Would you forgive the speaker?

_____

_____

Recognizing Style

Work with a partner to answer the questions.

1. What tells you that this is a poem?

    _____

    _____

2. What do you notice about the writer's use of lines and of punctuation?

    _____

    _____

3. How is this poem different from a traditional poem?

    _____

    _____

4. What kind of patterns can you see in the poem?

    _____

    _____

5. Read the poem aloud. Mark the places where you pause. Compare your answers with those of your partner. Decide which reading sounds best to you.

Discussion

Discuss these questions with your classmates.
1. Did you enjoy reading this poem? Why or why not?
2. Is it important to read poems? Why or why not?
3. Have you ever written poems? When and why?

Imagine that the poem was spoken as a conversation, instead of a poem. It might sound like this.

A: Who ate the plums that were in the icebox?

B: I did. I'm sorry.

A: I was saving them for breakfast. Why did you eat them?

B: They looked so sweet and so cold. They were delicious.

Read the following dialogues. Choose one that you like. Work with a partner. Try replacing some of the key words in the poem with words from the dialogue to make a new poem.

Dialogue 1

A: Who cut the rose from the rosebush that was in my garden?

B: I did. I'm sorry.

A: I waited so long for it to flower. I wanted to wear it to the dance on Saturday. Why did you do that?

B: It was so beautiful and had such a sweet smell. I wanted to have it.

Dialogue 2

A: Who crashed my new car, which was parked in my driveway? It was like my baby.

B: I did. I'm sorry.

A: I was going to drive it to work today. Why did you take it?

B: I wanted my friends to think it was mine.

Writing Practice

Write your own version of the poem using a different topic.

CHAPTER SIXTEEN

A Folktale

Pre-Reading Activity

Discuss these questions.

1. What are some famous folktales?
2. Why do people like them?
3. What is your favorite folktale?

Key Vocabulary

Do you know these words? Match the words with the meanings.

1. _____ famine   a. look at something briefly
2. _____ tent   b. desire to find out more about something
3. _____ glance   c. news that may or may not be true
4. _____ steam   d. a time when many people have no food
5. _____ curiosity   e. temporary shelter that a person can carry
6. _____ rumor   f. what rises into the air when water gets very hot

A   This story happened a long time ago, somewhere in Europe, in the middle of a bitter winter. There was a terrible **famine** throughout the land. In the villages, people were so hungry that each family kept their food hidden away, so that no one else would be able to find it. They hardly spoke to each other, and if any food was found, they fought over it.

B   One day, a poor traveler arrived in a village and set up his **tent** by the side of the road. He had with him a large pot, a wooden spoon, and a stone.

"You can't stay here," said the villagers. "There's no food for you!" And they raced back to their houses to make sure no one would steal their food while they were away.

"That doesn't matter," said the stranger. "I have everything I need."

He gathered sticks and built a fire in the middle of the main square. Then he placed his pot on the fire and added some water. He **glanced** around and noticed that he was being watched from every window and from every doorway. He smiled with satisfaction as the **steam** rose from the pot. Next, he took an ordinary stone from his pocket, which he carefully placed in the pot. He stirred the soup and waited patiently for it to boil.

C   By this time, the villagers were full of **curiosity**. Several of them had gathered around the pot. "What are you making?" they asked.

"Stone soup," replied the man. "It smells good, doesn't it?" And he sniffed the soup and smiled in anticipation. "Of course, a little salt and pepper would really help the flavor."

"I think I could find some salt and pepper," said one of the women, and she ran back to her house to fetch the salt and pepper to add to the soup.

"How tasty it would be with a tiny piece of garlic," said the traveler.

"I might have a tiny piece of garlic," said another villager.

"If only we had some potatoes, too, then it would really be delicious," said the stranger.

"I'll get you a potato," said another man and rushed home to fetch it.

D   Soon the **rumor** had spread around the whole village. Someone was making a delicious soup with a special stone. People came from every house to smell the bubbling soup, and each of them brought an extra ingredient to make the soup taste even better. They were so hungry, and the soup smelled so good. "It must be that special stone," they said.

Finally, the man declared that the soup was ready and it was time to eat. The villagers each brought a dish, and there was plenty of food for everyone. They talked and laughed, and for a while they forgot the famine and the cold. Even long after the famine had ended, people still remembered that night and the finest soup they had ever tasted.

Vocabulary

Meaning

Complete the sentences with the following words.

famine	tent
rumor	glanced
curiosity	steam

1. A ―――――― is a shelter that you can fold up and carry with you.

2. The news may be true, or it may just be a ――――――.

3. When there is no food in a country, there is a ――――――.

4. They asked a lot of questions because they could not control their ――――――.

5. He ―――――― at the book, but didn't look at it carefully.

6. When you boil water, you can see ――――――.

Vocabulary Activity

Answer the questions. Use complete sentences.

1. What can we do to prevent famines?

   _____

2. What kinds of rumors do you sometimes hear or see in the news?

   _____

3. Have you ever stayed in a tent? When? Where?

   _____

4. When you buy vegetables, do you just glance at them or do you look at them carefully?

   _____

5. What kinds of things make you curious?

   _____

6. What can steam be used for?

   _____

Comprehension

Understanding the Story

Write complete answers to these questions.

1. What was happening in the villages of the land?

   _____

2. Why were the villagers hiding their food?

   _____

3. Why were they unfriendly to the traveler?

   _____

4. Why were they curious about the stone soup?

   _____

5. What kind of man was the traveler?

   _____

6. How did he make the villagers share their food?

   _____

7. What was the traveler's trick?

   _____

8. Why would the villagers never forget the stone soup?

   _____

Interpreting the Story

Circle the letter of the best answer.

1. In the story, the villagers represent _____.
   a. people who think only of themselves
   b. people who work together
   c. people who are generous
   d. people who like to cook

2. In the story, the traveler represents _____.
   a. someone who helps people to work in a team
   b. someone who forces people to like each other
   c. someone who gives help when it is needed
   d. someone who prefers to be alone

3. In the story, the soup represents _____.
   a. something everyone wants but can't have
   b. something everyone can make individually
   c. something everyone can make together
   d. something everyone hates

4. What is the moral (the lesson) of the story?
   a. Everyone can be successful if he or she wants.
   b. No one is better than anyone else.
   c. People can achieve more by helping each other.
   d. Think before you act.

Recognizing Style

Work with a partner to answer the questions.

1. What tells you that this is a folktale?

   _____

2. Are the characters in the story realistic? Why or why not?

   _____

3. The story has four parts. Match each part with one of the descriptions below. Which part describes each of the following?
   _____ Mysterious events that make the reader curious
   _____ The setting for the story
   _____ A happy conclusion to the story
   _____ The meaning of the mysterious events

4. Does the story use a direct or indirect method of presenting its main meaning? Do you think this is effective? Why or why not?

   _____

Discussion

Discuss these questions with your classmates.
1. How did you learn about folktales in your culture?
2. Do you think that folktales are important? How important are they, and why?
3. Are folktales less important today than they were in the past? Why?
4. What can we learn from folktales, and how useful are they in our daily lives?

Work with a partner. Think of a situation where people have to work together to create something. Make a list of three or four such situations. Now retell the story of stone soup in a modern setting, using one of these situations.

Exercise 1

Find the mistakes. There are 10 mistakes in grammar, punctuation, capitalization, and spelling. Find and correct them.

> The old Queen wanted to find out whether the girl was a real
>
> Princess. So she goes to the bedrom took all the bedding off the bed
>
> and put a pea on the bottom. Then, she took twenty mattresses and
>
> put it on top of pea. Finally she put twenty feather beds on top of
>
> the mattresses.

Writing Practice

1. Read the story again and underline all the adjectives—for example, *in the middle of a <u>bitter</u> winter.* Notice how these words help to create a vivid picture.

2. Work in pairs. Read the paragraph below. What kinds of adjectives can you add to make the story more interesting? Add as many adjectives as you can and rewrite the paragraph. Read your version to the rest of the class.

A long time ago, in a <u>distant</u> country, a _____ girl lived with her

_____ stepmother and two _____ stepsisters. Her _____

mother was dead, and her _____ father had married again. The

_____ wife and her two _____ daughters hated the _____

stepdaughter and forced her to wear _____ clothes and do all

kinds of _____ work around the _____ house. One day, a

_____ letter arrived in the mail. . . .

3. How does the story continue? Write your own ending.
4. Think of folktales you know. Write the first line and the last line. See if your group can guess the story.

Do you know these famous books?

Match the following book titles to the descriptions given below. Can you name the authors of these books?

_____ 1. A story about a group of sailors who go out to hunt an enormous whale.

_____ 2. A story about a man who goes sailing alone and catches a big fish.

_____ 3. A story about a famous London detective who solves his cases by using logic.

_____ 4. A dramatic story of love and death, set in the American Civil War.

_____ 5. A story describing a future world where individual lives are controlled by the state.

_____ 6. A story about a doctor who experiments with creating a new kind of human.

a. *The Adventures of Sherlock Holmes*

b. *Gone with the Wind*

c. *Moby Dick*

d. *The Old Man and the Sea*

e. *Frankenstein*

f. *1984*

Video Activity • The Poetry of e. e. cummings   CNN

e. e. (Edward Estlin) cummings was born in Cambridge, Massachusetts, in 1894 and died in 1962. He wrote twelve volumes of poetry and is one of America's most popular modern poets. The video talks about his life and work.

1. First viewing: Watch the video and make notes about the following:
   a. What facts do you learn about e. e. cummings' life?
   b. What is included in this exhibition?
   c. What are the titles of some of his poetry collections?
2. Second viewing: Watch the video again. What does the video tell you about e. e. cummings' poetry? What makes it unusual? What do you notice about the way it looks on the page?
3. Now write a short summary of what you learned about e. e. cummings and his poetry.

Internet Activity

Think of a famous folktale from your country. Go to the Internet to find a website with the story. Read the story. Are there any differences between the way you remember the story and the way it is told on the Internet?

Expanding a Paragraph into an Essay

Sample Student Paragraph

⬭	
	Learning a Foreign Language
Topic sentence becomes thesis statement.	There are a lot of processes to go through in order to learn
Support sentence 1	a foreign language. First, you have to like the people who speak
Support sentence 2	that language. Then you have to find either a tutor or a teacher
Support sentence 3	to help you with the language. After finding a person to teach
⬭	you that language, you must work hard to understand what he
Conclusion sentence	or she is teaching you. In conclusion, I think learning a foreign
	language is very useful and a lot of fun.

Sample Student Essay

	Learning a Foreign Language
Introduction	Learning a foreign language can be fun and interesting. You can hear and understand what people from other countries are saying. It feels good knowing what others are talking about. It is
Thesis statement	not easy learning a different language. There are a lot of processes to go through in order to learn a foreign language.
Body paragraph 1	First, you have to like the people who speak that language. You have to know the culture and the people. It makes learning less complicated. For example, I really like French music, and I want to understand the words of the songs. Then you have a reason to start learning the language.
Body paragraph 2	Then you have to find either a tutor or a teacher to help you with the language. You can do that by contacting some schools or asking your advisor. Having friends who speak that language can be very nice, too. They can help you to know that language out of class. For example, I can go to a French movie with a French friend and then talk about it.
Body paragraph 3	After finding a person to teach you that language, you must work hard to understand what he or she is teaching you. Make sure you ask questions if you have any problems. When you are comfortable talking and writing that language is when I think you have accomplished your goal.
Conclusion	In conclusion, I think learning a foreign language is very useful and a lot of fun. It helps you a lot in finding a job. It makes you feel smart knowing what others might not know. Learning a language can be fascinating and thrilling. Who knows what you can do with that language!

Answer Key

Unit 1: Do you know these interesting facts about the brain?
1. T   2. F   3. F   4. F   5. T   6. F   7. T

Unit 2: Do you know these interesting facts about food?
1. T   2. F   3. T   4. F   5. T   6. F   7. T   8. F
9. T   10. T

Unit 3: Do you know about these American customs and traditions?
1. T   2. F   3. F   4. F   5. T   6. T   7. T   8. F

Unit 4: Who are they?
1. Abraham Lincoln   2. Mozart   3. Martin Luther King, Jr.
4. Helen Keller   5. Mother Teresa   6. Mary Shelley

Unit 5: What do you know about insects?
1. b   2. b   3. a   4. b   5. b   6. a   7. a   8. b
9. b   10. b

Unit 6: Inventions quiz
1. a   2. a   3. c   4. b   5. c   6. b   7. a   8. c

Unit 7: Do you know about these laws?
1. T   2. T   3. F   4. F   5. F   6. T   7. T

Unit 8: Do you know these famous books?
1. c; *Moby Dick,* by Herman Melville   2. d; *The Old Man and the Sea,* by Ernest Hemingway   3. a; *The Adventures of Sherlock Holmes,* by Arthur Conan Doyle   4. b; *Gone with the Wind,* by Margaret Mitchell   5. f; *1984,* by George Orwell
6. e; *Frankenstein,* by Mary Shelley

Skills Index

Grammar and Usage

Clauses
  Dependent clauses, 72–74
  Main clauses, 72–74
Conjunctions
  Coordinating conjunctions, 21–24
Nouns
  Proper nouns, 10–12
Pronouns, 9
Time and place expressions, 111–113

Listening/Speaking

Discussion, 2, 7, 15, 20, 27, 30, 34, 41, 46,
    56, 60, 66, 70, 77–78, 80, 85, 90, 94,
    104, 109, 115, 119, 128, 132, 139, 143,
    154, 159, 166, 171, 180, 183, 185, 191
Listening to selections, 3–4, 16–17, 31–32,
    42–43, 57–58, 67–68, 81–82, 91–92,
    105–106, 116–117, 129–130, 140–141,
    155–156, 167–168, 181, 186–187
Pre-reading activities, 2, 15, 30, 41, 56,
    66, 80, 90, 104, 115, 128, 139, 154,
    166, 180, 185

Reading

Comprehension, 6, 19–20, 33–34, 45,
    60–61, 69–71, 84–85, 93–94, 108–109,
    118–119, 131–132, 143, 158–159,
    170–171, 182–183, 189–190
Literary forms
  Folktale, 186–187
  Informational text, 3–4, 16–17, 31–32,
    42–43, 57–58, 67–68, 81–82, 91–92,
    105–106, 116–117, 129–130, 140–141,
    155–156, 167–168
  Poetry, 181

Pre-reading activities, 2, 15, 30, 41, 56,
    66, 80, 90, 104, 115, 128, 139, 154,
    166, 180, 185
Recognizing style, 183, 190–191
Vocabulary, 2–5, 15–18, 30–32, 41–44,
    56–59, 66–69, 80–83, 90–93, 104–107,
    115–118, 128–131, 139–142, 154–157,
    166–169, 180–182, 185–188

Technology—Internet

Astrology, 28
Customs, 78
Famous people, 102
Folktales, 193
Inventions, 152
Laws, 178
Natural disasters, 126
Unusual foods, 54

Test-Taking Skills

Matching, 2, 15, 30, 41, 56, 66, 80, 90, 104,
    115, 128, 139, 154, 166, 180, 185, 193
Multiple-choice questions, 6, 19, 33, 45,
    48–49, 60, 69–70, 84, 93–94, 108, 119,
    125–126, 132, 142–143, 151, 158, 170,
    190
Open-ended questions, 5, 11–12, 18, 44,
    59, 60–61, 68–69, 70–71, 83, 107,
    108–109, 118, 119–120, 131–132, 142,
    157, 169, 182–183, 188, 189, 190–191
Sentence completion, 4, 17–18, 32, 43,
    58–59, 68, 82, 92, 106, 117, 130–131,
    135–136, 141, 156–157, 168–169, 181,
    187
True/false questions, 6, 19–20, 26, 27, 45,
    53, 77, 94, 143, 158–159, 170–171, 177

Word completion, 93

Topics

Viewing

Writing and Mechanics